IN TRUTH AND LOVE

by

The Rt. Rev. William Gordon Wheeler
M.A. (Oxon), Hon. D.D. (Leeds)
Bishop Emeritus of Leeds

Assisted by Robert E. Finnigan, M. Phil.

Catholic Media Office

GOWLAND & CO

Published for and on behalf of
The Rt Rev Wm Gordon Wheeler
by
Gowland & Co.,
93 Bedford Road,
Birkdale, Southport,
Merseyside, PR8 4HT

© Wm Gordon Wheeler 1990
First printed 1990
Reprinted 1991

ISBN 1 872480 09 8

All rights reserved. No part of this publication may be reproduced, stored in a retrieval system, or transmitted in any form, or by any means, electronic, mechanical, photocopying or otherwise without the written permission of the publisher.

Produced in Great Britain by
Gowland & Co.,
Southport, Merseyside

To My Sister
Marjorie Elizabeth Easton

CONTENTS

Introduction	A Span of Eighty Years	9
Chapter I	Towards a Fullness of Faith	13
Chapter II	The Years of Priesthood	39
Chapter III	The Years of Episcopate	80
Chapter IV	The Shape of Things to Come?	141
Epilogue		150
Index		152

WHEN as a child I laughed and wept,
Time crept.
When as a youth I dreamed and talked,
Time walked.
When I became a full - grown man,
Time ran;
And later when I grew older,
Time flew.
Soon I shall find, while travelling on,
Time gone.
May Christ have saved my soul by then.
Amen.

Lines
found on
an old bell
at Chester

By kind permission of Stanbrook Abbey, Worcester.

A SPAN OF EIGHTY YEARS

As I approach my eightieth birthday many of my friends have asked me to write some reflections, especially on fifty years of Priesthood and twenty-five of Episcopacy, which might in some way be of help to others. Perhaps however before I go any further, I ought to tell you something of the main events of these eighty years.

I was born on the 5th May 1910 to Frederick and Marjorie Wheeler (nee Upjohn) in the village of Dobcross near Saddleworth, which was in those days part of the West Riding of Yorkshire. The family moved shortly afterwards to Greenfield and it was there that my only sister, Marjorie Elizabeth (who has always been known as Betty), was born. When the 1914 war broke out, as my father was likely to be called up, we returned to my mother's part of the world and when the time came for my father to go to the war we were soon afterwards taken by my mother to live with her father and mother at Worsley in Lancashire. There I had a memorable and extremely happy childhood in the midst of a patriarchal family. For whilst my paternal grandfather had only eight children, my maternal grandfather had sixteen, many of whom often gathered at his home at weekends. My grandfather's home was in unspoilt country on what was then the estate of Lord Ellesmere.

After going to Prep Schools at Swinton and Eccles, I graduated to Manchester Grammar School and was there until I went to Oxford in 1929. These school days were very happy ones. I ultimately became a prefect at the MGS which brought certain privileges such as spending a lot of time in the John Rylands Library in Manchester. Proceeding to University College, I first of all read History and was awarded an Exhibition; this was continued after I had taken my degree and allowed me to do Theology. About the same time my parents moved to Sussex. There we lived at Montague, Hankham, a lovely old farmhouse, which was to be my home for the next ten years.

My mother's family were devout Anglicans and I was brought up in an atmosphere of Faith for which I am always grateful. There were clergy on both sides of the family and accordingly it was quite in the line of tradition that I should proceed to Holy Orders in the Church of England, and so I went on to St Stephen's House, Oxford. I was eventually ordained deacon by Bishop George Bell of Chichester and priest by the Bishop of Derby. The vicar to whom I had been assigned took me from St Bartholomew's, Brighton to Our Lady and All Saints, Chesterfield, the church with the crooked spire, and from there I went to be an assistant Chaplain at Lancing College in Sussex. It was from Lancing that I went to Downside Abbey in the Autumn of 1936 to be received into the Catholic Church. In 1986 I went back to say a Mass of Thanksgiving in the Lady Chapel at Downside. That was a Golden Jubilee which I spent happily with the Abbot and the monks.

From Downside in 1936 I went straight to Rome to study for the priesthood, having been sponsored by Cardinal Hinsley for the Diocese of Westminster and having had my fees paid by a good friend who had taken the same step as myself. She had the joy before she died of seeing me ordained to the priesthood in the crypt of Westminster Cathedral on March 31st 1940 and being present at my first Mass in the Slipper Chapel at Walsingham on the following day. It happened that year to be the transferred feast of the Annunciation. I had been in Rome from '36 -'39 at the Beda College which was then in the Via san Nicolo da Tolentino near the Piazza Barberini. After the war the college was moved to a new site and a new building on land presented by Pope Pius XII belonging to the Vatican opposite the facade of St Paul's Outside the Walls. In 1939 when the war broke out we were unable to return to Rome from vacation and were accommodated for the remaining year of preparation in St Joseph's College, Upholland in Lancashire.

In the summer of 1940 I was appointed Curate at St Edmund's, Lower Edmonton in North London and was there through the worst of the war years. But in 1944 I was moved to Westminster Cathedral to be a chaplain there and to edit the Westminster Cathedral Chronicle. I did this for six years and then was asked by Cardinal Griffin to become chaplain to the Catholics in the University of London. I continued that until 1954 when the same Cardinal summoned me to become the Administrator of Westminster Cathedral. This was an assignment that I held for ten years with great happiness. It was in 1964 that I was asked to go as Coadjutor to the Bishop of Middlesbrough. I was consecrated by Archbishop Cardinale who was then the Apostolic Delegate in this country, on March 19th of that year in the old Cathedral at Middlesbrough, and had a very happy two and a half years living within sight of the lovely Cleveland Hills. I had made my pre-consecration retreat at Ampleforth and had been accompanied by the Abbot on the way up from London. Little did he or I think in those days that he would become one day Archbishop of Westminster and a Cardinal. It was the beginning of a close friendship for which I am always grateful. Subsequently, I was appointed Bishop of Leeds because my predecessor had been transferred to the metropolitan See of Birmingham. I was sorry to have had so short a time in the Middlesbrough Diocese especially as a great part of it was spent in Rome at the Second Vatican Council. But this, as you can imagine, was one of the great and most valued experiences of my life. For nineteen years I held the See of Leeds to my utmost ability and became very devoted to the priests and people, ever remaining so and filled with admiration for their goodness. In 1985, having reached the canonical age of seventy-five for retirement, I submitted my resignation to Pope John Paul II and came to live in the College of the Blessed Virgin Mary at Headingley under the caring umbrella of the Little Sisters of the Poor.

As one gets older one sees the pattern of one's life and is more and more filled with gratitude to God for all His goodness and the caring of His Divine Providence. Of course in all our lives there have been many sorrows and sadnesses but all in all I am filled with joy and gratitude when I think of all the wonderful people that I have known and loved and all the lovely things that have happened to me. Many friendships remain and I am kept quite busy in my retirement which I understand is the best thing that can happen at this stage of one's life.

You will think I have given you a thumb-nail sketch with very little comment. I have done this purposely so that you have the total picture so far as my eightieth year. Later on I shall hope to expand on some of the different experiences of my life not forgetting that I have been asked to give some helpful and encouraging words to others. This is my purpose: whether I succeed or not the reader alone can be the judge.

I should like to say, however, that despite all my good resolutions I never really got down to these reminiscences until others came to the rescue. My successor, Bishop David Konstant, who so kindly commissioned the portrait by Andrew Festing, had appointed Robert Finnigan, a young historian who had recently published a quite notable monograph on St. Anne's Cathedral, Leeds, as assistant archivist of the diocese. I had met him once at Eltofts when he was cataloguing, with high efficiency, a lot of papers relating to the sixties and seventies. Subsequently, Fr. Arthur Roche, who had been one of my secretaries, and to whom I owe a great debt of gratitude, suggested that Robert Finnigan should help me with this work, asking me some questions, arranging the typing of my musings - which has been done very proficiently by Mrs Denise Ibbetson - and preparing the way for their possible publication. Over the past year he has spent many hours with me week by week. His friendship, no less that his efficiency, has meant a great deal to me and he deserves all the credit for an achievement which, left alone, could never have been mine.

+ Wm. Gordon Wheeler

TOWARDS A FULLNESS OF FAITH

R.E.F.:
My Lord, you have already told us in your introduction about your Anglican upbringing and that it was not until you were twenty-six years of age that you became a Roman Catholic. With hindsight, of course, we can see how this event marks the most important turning point in your life. Perhaps we could begin, therefore, with your thoughts on how and when the 'Pilgrimage of Faith' which led you to the Church of Rome began?

The Bishop:
When I was about nine years old there came to St Mark's, Worsley a new Vicar. His name was H. W. Thorne, in later years a Canon of Rochester. I well remember the stir that his appointment caused when it was known that he was of pronounced Anglo-Catholic sympathies. I remember too attending the inauguration of what to me, as indeed it was to many of far riper age, an entirely new service. For after a short instruction High Matins were abolished in favour of the Holy Eucharist. At Sunday dinner it was discussed with that frankness and bitterness which usually characterised religious debates in those days. My Aunt Ida was the only protagonist of the new regime which was anathema to the rest of the family, including as far as I can remember my own parents. Apparently, when the Parthian shots had been delivered on both sides, I, to the surprise of both parties said "Well I think it is the most beautiful service I have ever seen."

The loyalty of the family to the Parish Church of Worsley overrode, however, all other considerations and their dislike of the Thorne regime in its beginnings did not prevent my attending the Sung Eucharist and Catechism each Sunday. When my father went to the War our own home was closed and my mother and sister and I went to live with my maternal grandparents and various aunts. It was through this move that I came under the aegis religiously of my Aunt Ida. She saw that my sister and I attended the Parish Church assiduously and of course my mother happily concurred. From Mr Thorne I learnt the first elements of the Catholic Faith and I could never be sufficiently grateful to him for all his teaching and help. Before I reached the age of twelve I was prepared by him for Confirmation and received the Laying-on of hands from the Bishop of Blackburn in February 1922. Thereafter I was his first altar boy and served regularly twice each Sunday morning.

> *About this time you left your preparatory school at Eccles and became a pupil at Manchester Grammar School. How did your introduction to Anglo-Catholicism affect your school life?*

My interest in religion generally undoubtedly affected my schoolwork. My essays for some reason almost invariably seemed to take a religious or ecclesiastical turn. If the subject was Bathing, Books or Bicycles the Almighty turned up at the beginning or the end with a frequency which must have been exasperating to some of those who had to teach me. And indeed I remember Mr Hyslop, my second Form Master at MGS. saying "Really William Gordon, this is getting as bad as Mr Dick in David Copperfield!" I think I was rather upset at the time and longed for the more sympathetic line of Mr Woodcock, my first Form Master. From the start he was a great friend to me and became my first and greatest hero. He had been a Fellow of St John's, Oxford and was a formidable classical scholar and an athlete and a Wesleyan! He was a firm disciplinarian: but like all real disciplinarians a man of unbounded sympathies. He was what we would have called a 'Tough' at Oxford: but he was a scholarly 'Tough' and had a deep and serious religious background. It was he who encouraged me in the idea of taking Holy Orders.

At the same time I found myself at school as the protagonist of the Anglo-Catholic line, and this attachment came to play quite a part in my school life. I can remember during this period, about 1926, there was a school trip to Paris, my first journey abroad. We went to stay in the Lycee de St Michel in the Latin Quarter and were taken all round the usual sights. During this visit, on Easter Sunday, we went to High Mass in Notre Dame. It was the first time I had been in a Catholic church, and therefore the first time I had been to Mass. Cardinal Dubois, the Archbishop of Paris, was pontificating and I was swept off my feet by the ceremonial. I always remember the school master who was with us, a wonderful man called H. F. Collins, gave a whispered running commentary on what he thought was happening. As Cardinal Dubois came down, at the end, in procession, he was accompanied by a whole suite of clerical attendants. I realise now that these were the Canons of Notre Dame in their Canonical robes. I said to Mr Collins "Who are all these old gentlemen?" "Those," he answered, "are his six Jesuit confessors." I thought what a wicked old man he must be to need all those. Again the master whispered to me and said "They always make-up these Cardinals in these processions. Just look at him very closely as he comes by and you will see that". This, I think, he really believed. I can remember for ever afterwards thinking that this scene was one of the most remarkable things I had ever witnessed and when I got back to England, to the great annoyance of the family, I went on a long tram car ride from Worsley Court House to Salford, and the only Catholic church that I knew existed. It was Salford Cathedral and in those days it seemed very strange to me because I had only been used to people going to church very well dressed for the occasion. But in this Cathedral when I went in, I found it packed with people: with men with rags around their necks and women with shawls and clogs and I had never seen people like that in a church before. I remember looking at the Holy Water stoop and thinking it must be some sort of Baptismal Font and finding it full of dirt - it was all very unhygienic. I attended the Mass there and again I thought how wonderful this is because the people of God, so to speak, are here: it's not just the well dressed. I never saw anybody in Worsley parish church who wasn't in their Sunday best, including me!

> *At the age of sixteen you chose to stay on at M.G.S. rather than start a career in commerce or one of the professions. At that point you entered the school's History Sixth and it was from there that you went up to University College, Oxford in 1929 to read for a degree in History. For an Anglo-Catholic such as yourself what did going to Oxford mean at that time?*

When I got to Oxford, I found Anglo-Catholicism in excelsis. When I was instructed by Canon Thorne I was taught about confession, but I'd never been allowed by my parents to go to confession. When I went to Oxford as a 19 year old I made my first confession to an Anglican clergyman and this was a great event. I used to get up every morning and go to the Anglican Eucharist in Pusey House in Oxford, and used to serve it. In my first year I was a sacristan there. The Librarians, as they were called, were four clergy and a wonderful old principal called Dr Darwell Stone. He was a great Patristic scholar. I used to go to confession to him, a marvellous old gentleman with a white beard. They were all very kind to me. There was one particularly so, Canon Frederic Hood who became a close friend and inspiration all the time I was at Oxford. I very much made Pusey House my spiritual home but I used to go to the other Anglo-Catholic churches as well like the Cowley Fathers, St Barnabas', St Paul's, St Mary Magdalene's and others. So one grew up in that sort of atmosphere. One got all the satisfaction of the full sacramental system and the beauty of worship and music and so forth in the High Anglican set up. But, I did go to the Dominicans in Blackfriars to listen especially to the lectures on St Thomas Aquinas. And I used to go to St Aloysius for Benediction. But we even had Benediction in Pusey House, St Paul's and places like that.

Why did you choose to study history as an undergraduate?

History has always been my first love, from being at prep. school. I have always been fascinated by history and all the books I had as a child were history books. This is something I have never lost. Even now if I have got to preach a sermon I think of the historical side of it before the theological one. My history course at Oxford encompassed English history from the ninth century to modern times. There were all sorts of special subjects, Industrial Relations in the nineteenth century for example. I spent countless hours in the Radcliffe Camera reading Bluebooks and that sort of thing, but my favourite period was always the sixteenth century, where I was always more interested in the Counter Reformation than the Reformation itself.

This was a very happy time for me indeed during which I made a great many friends. At the end of my course I got a very good second and therefore they continued the little Exhibition I had been awarded since the second year. I was asked to do the Honours School of Theology after my degree and I proceeded to do that because it fitted in with preparation for the ministry, which had to be combined with residence in a theological college in the city .

Academically this was a great mistake. Looking back I think it is unwise to attempt in one year a second Honours School unless one is outstandingly brilliant. I was already entirely disenchanted with the Anglican situation. And added to that I was passing through perhaps the lowest trough in my life and perhaps near to a nervous breakdown. I was certainly not in a mood to tackle the syllabus in the way I should have done and the result in the Schools was disastrous. It was in fact surprising that I scraped through in the lowest category. My tutor, Dr Kirk, was very taken aback and so were my other friends and advisers. Retrospectively I think I let them down rather badly. Perhaps it is a good thing to have known failure in one's life!

What do you recall of the personalities you encountered at Oxford?

When I first went up to Univ (University College, Oxford) in 1929, the college chaplain was a very venerable figure, Dr A. J. Carlyle. He must also have been very old because he was somewhat forgetful: and I can remember his inserting in the prayer for the Royal Family "Adelaide our Queen Dowager." He was also supposed to be the original of the story of the Ten Commandments, recited on occasions in the Anglican Communion Service. A Don who was exhausted by the setting and marking of too many examination papers, is reported to have added, after the tenth, "Candidates are requested only to attempt seven of these."

I can remember his preaching a sermon on the Fall of Man insisting that far from being due to Sin, it marked the beginning of Enlightenment. This roused a volume of response from the Lady Margaret Professor of Divinity, who wrote a classic treatise on the subject. He himself was an interesting cleric who, it was said, before his marriage had written a Tract on the advantages of Celibacy. It was also said that he and his wife spent their honeymoon touring round buying up copies from church Tract cases and making a huge bonfire. It was said too that he was at a loss where communication with small babes was concerned. He had been observed waking up his first-born in the pram outside his door in Tom Quad with the words: "Wake up, Theodore, I wish to introduce you to the Regius Professor of Divinity."

The Master of Univ. at that time was Sir Michael Sadler, a notable figure also in Leeds. In the customary way I was invited as a Fresher to take breakfast with him in The Master's Lodging where he showed us his large collection of modern art. When I persuaded a clerical post-graduate student from Australia to celebrate the Eucharist daily in the College Chapel one Lent, the Master supported it with his presence every day. That student was Allen Winter who subsequently became Bishop of Melbourne. And when he came to the Lambeth Conference in 1960, I entertained him at Westminster Cathedral.

The Dean of the College was Sir David Lindsay Keir, an impressive and delightful man, who later became the Vice Chancellor of Queen's University, Belfast and subsequently Master of Balliol. He was my Tutor in Constitutional History. As Dean, he was also responsible for discipline: as I knew on one occasion to my cost. I had lovely rooms above his, looking on the Inner Quad, and had the misfortune, in experimenting with pipe-smoking, to set a cushion on fire. It was night time and so thoughtlessly I flung it out of the window. Next morning, Harry Green, my "Scout" who was a model "Jeeves", drew my bedroom curtains and turned round to my bed saying: "The Dean's compliments, Sir, and he wishes to see you immediately." "Good gracious, Harry," I said, "what can I have done." "I think," he said "that if you look out of your window, Sir, you will realise." I leapt out of bed and there was the beautiful grass, nurtured for hundreds of years, heavily marked with the burning stuffing of that cushion. I discovered later that some "drunks" had come through the Quad and had a game of football with it.

Of course, I apologised to the Dean but I had such a wigging, in unsurpassable prose, as I shall never forget. I was threatened with being 'sent down' for irresponsibility, or at least 'rusticated', and threatened with a fine of £50. Eventually I got away with a fiver. Even that was a small fortune in those days. Sir David evidently did not hold it against me because he recommended me for a closed Exhibition in History shortly afterwards and thirty years later congratulated me on becoming a Bishop.

I found it much more difficult to communicate easily with my next two tutors: Kenneth Leys in History and the Rev Dr Grensted in Theology. I am sure this was my fault. Quite wrongly, I was frightened of Leys, and I was intolerant of Grensted's churchmanship. All this was redeemed in having Kenneth Kirk, the Chaplain of Trinity, and later Bishop of Oxford, as my final theology tutor. He was a theologian of the highest integrity and catholically minded.

I had many other friends among the clergy of those days. I have already spoken of the great Patristic scholar, Dr Darwell Stone who was the Principal of Pusey House. He was also famous for rather ingenious remarks. One day at table some contemporary stage artists known as the Dolly Sisters came into the conversation. Darwell said "The Dolly Sisters? I haven't heard of that community before." I once asked at luncheon there, somewhat naively, why a certain curate in Oxford was known as the L.G.C. It was explained to me that the letters stood for the "Lowest of God's Creatures". And Darwell added to that information: "It doesn't refer to his stature." There were no flies on him. The four Librarians on his staff were all friends of mine: Freddy Hood, who ultimately succeeded Darwell as Principal and later became a Canon of St Paul's; Miles Sargent; Humphrey Beevor, who later became a Bishop in Africa; and Leslie Cross, who became a Regius Professor. With other friends I had some interesting holidays especially with Freddy and Humphrey and they initiated me into the London scene of Anglo-Catholicism.

It was through Pusey House that I also met Billy Clonmore (later Lord Wicklow) when he was an Anglican Deacon. He later became a Catholic and helped me a great deal. When I 'Poped', he acted as my Godparent at Confirmation. I had in later years many happy times in his lovely home near the James Joyce Tower in Dun Laoghaire. When Lord Clonmore first became a Catholic his father, the old Lord Wicklow, told him not to come home to Sheldon Manor at weekends because he did not consider it *comme il faut* for him to be seen going off with the Servants Hall to the Mass. I still see Billy's widow, Eleanor Wicklow, when I go to Ireland.

Then there was that wonderful 18th century figure, the Reverend Bartle Hack, Vicar of St Mary Magdalene's by the side of Balliol off the Corn. That Church was known then as The Archipelago because it had so many 'aisles'. Mr Hack was very portly. He lived in a house next door to Blackwells, (now pulled down I think) and it was said that he found the hill up The Broad rather much for him. His dinner parties were very select. A regular visitor and great friend was the old bachelor Duke of Argyll. It was said that he believed in fairies and dressed like an old farmer. But he was very good company. I once met Mr Hack in the Corn. "Ah, master Wheeler," he said "come home with me for a dish o tay." I replied that I had already had tea. "Where did you take it, Master Wheeler?" he said. I replied "In Elliston and Cavells, Mr Hack." "In my day" rejoined Mr Hack, "no gentleman would take tea at anywhere but Boffins." He was a lovable and most edifying cleric.

Another character was Roger Wodehouse of the Kimberley family, Vicar of St Paul's. He was more Roman than Anglican and his church reflected it. There was a very beautiful shrine of Our Lady in his church and on her feast day in October, his mother would send up her jewels from the bank vaults and the statue was bedecked and carried around with jangling ear-rings and other jewels worth a Kings Ransom. Would it be safe to do such a thing today?

Dr B. J. Kidd, the Warden of Keble was likewise very catholically-minded but far less extreme. He would wear a mortar-board rather than a biretta. He endeared himself to me because I used to go to his study for sessions of a small group who like myself were working on 'Reformation and Counter-Reformation' as a special subject. On his desk he had a magnificent signed photograph of Cardinal Mercier who initiated the Malines Conversations with the then Lord Halifax. And Dr Kidd had been present at the original sessions. I remember him preaching in Pusey House from a script during which there were pauses whilst he took out his pen and made alterations. It was described afterwards by one of the Librarians "as a try-out for the provinces." I have always been intrigued by eccentrics.

Then there was the Rev E. C. Ratcliff, Chaplain in those days at The Queen's College. He combined his vocation with a high appreciation of civilisation and a continental outlook. He entertained all his friends most lavishly, again in 18th century rather than 20th century style. He was a liturgical scholar and a mine of information regarding a wide range of rites. I remember once that he outraged the more advanced Anglo-Catholics by preaching a University Sermon in favour liturgically of the 1928 revision of the Book of Common Prayer. In those days that subject was as divisive in the Church of England as the question of women priests today. *"Plus ca change plus c'est la meme chose."*

Many other interesting personalities came my way: Clara Harriet Browne, for example. She lived in a house on the Iffley Road and had a private chapel with a relic of the True Cross. She gave coffee and compline parties; much more edifying than the cocktail variety. One met many friends there - Dr Tom Parker, I think was one of them and he in much later days became Chaplain of Univ. When the then Vice-Chancellor in the late sixties - he was Provost of Oriel, - invited me for the first time as a Catholic Bishop to preach the University Sermon in St Mary's, dear Tom was amongst the robed Doctors of Divinity who attended and escorted me afterwards to All Souls for refreshment. Miss Browne became a Catholic a short time after I did and was instructed and received by the Dominicans.

Of course, my greatest friends in Oxford days were my own contemporaries: Bertram Barnes of Magdalene, Patrick McLaughlin of Worcester, Hugh Frazer of Univ and his brother James of New College. Then there was Martin Gibbs also of Univ. and my old school friends David Peck, Reginald Cadman and Noel Renshaw. Most of them became Anglican clergymen and when I became Bishop of Leeds I found Hugh Woodall of Keble as Vicar of Boston Spa. There were many others who played their different parts in my growth: friends such as Derek White of St Catherine's who died as a student at the Beda, Kenneth Boulton Jones who became an Anglican naval chaplain, and a Catholic friend Michael Riddle who, happily, was present in 1989 at my Silver Jubilee of Epsicopate. Many of them have already gone to God. I became aware how few are now left when I celebrated the Requiem recently in Ely Place for Patrick McLaughlin RIP. In their very different ways, I felt enriched by all of them, God bless them.

What about the Catholic figures you met at Oxford?

Let me tell you of the first Catholic Priest I ever met. It was Fr Martin D'Arcy SJ, the Master of Campion Hall. I was a member of the OUDS (Oxford University Dramatic Society) and I invited him to dinner there. It was an interesting stage in a friendship which matured later. For when I was made Chaplain to the Catholics of the University of London in 1950, and had to find and furnish a chaplaincy, he gave me a very lovely picture of the Tintoretto School for the reredos of the Chapel at 13, Devonshire Place. It depicted Our Lord's baptism and I often wonder where it is now. I remember about that time also visiting Fr D'Arcy in the new Campion Hall, built by Lutyens. In the Refectory he showed me a portrait of himself when he was Master there by Augustus John. At first sight it was a little startling and made me think of "sea-green Robespierre". Accordingly I was silent. And then I heard his well-known and very incisive voice behind me saying: "And that is the finest thing that Augustus John has ever done." Whilst I venerated his academic wisdom, I always found him somewhat enigmatic and beyond my ken. I was told by another Jesuit subsequently that Augustus John had put the whole history of the Jesuit Order into that picture.

We certainly cannot leave the Oxford scene in the late twenties and early thirties without recording the late Monsignor Ronald Knox's long period as Catholic Chaplain to the undergraduates. My memories of him at that time are brief because, as you know already, I was not a Catholic in my undergraduate or early graduate days. I was often fascinated, however, by seeing him walking very slowly in Christ Church Meadows in the afternoon reciting his Breviary. My main memory of that time, however, was of one night when I went to his Chaplaincy with some Catholic friends to hear him read a paper on 'The Man who tried to convert the Pope.' He sat on the fire-guard in his very crowded study, pipe and manuscript in hand and with his gift for satire tempered by charity told us of a book published by a Canon of Durham entitled *Journal of a Tour in Italy in 1850*. The highlight of this was an Audience with Pope Pius IX in which the formidable Mrs Townsend acted as interpreter. It was one of the funniest things to which I have ever listened and I was delighted to find in later years that it had been preserved and published in a book that came out from Sheed and Ward in 1942 entitled *For Hilaire Belloc* (celebrating the author's 72nd birthday).

Later on, in my Catholic days, I got to know Ronnie very well and appreciated him ever increasingly. We had many gets together in the London Chaplaincy in the early fifties and in fact he preached for me at the inauguration of the Academic Mass in

St Etheldreda's, Ely Place. Often I saw him too in my Westminster Cathedral days. I still think of him as a very holy man, and well remember the great throngs at his Requiem in Westminster and later on the peacefulness of his last resting place at Mells in Somerset and near to Downside where I also visited him.

Did any of our Oxford friendships have a particular influence on your 'Pilgrimage of Faith'?

One friend of mine, in those days, was the Anglican Canon Herman Leonard Pass. He was the principal of Chichester Theological College, but I knew him chiefly through friends in Eastbourne where his own family lived. Canon Pass invited me, at one stage, to go, really as his secretary, all expenses paid, to the Conference of Theologians of Eastern and Western Churches at Berne in Switzerland. It was an extremely fascinating experience because ecumenically one met very well known world figures like Archbishop Soderblom of Uppsala, Sweden; Carl Ludwig Schmidt of Germany, Martin Dibelius of Germany and many others. Canon Pass was, I think, the only Anglican representative. One evening I was very intrigued to meet Nicolai Arseniev who was a Russian, and once again a very well-known ecumenical figure. He became a very close friend in later years. One evening the conference had a kind of get together where they all recounted some of the most interesting memories of their life and I think I am right in saying that the best contribution, or the one that impressed the most, was given by Canon Pass. He recounted to them how when he was studying some Hebrew document in the Ambrosian Library in Milan, the then Librarian was the man who subsequently became Pope Pius XI. He then spoke of the great kindness and attention that he had received in that library. This experience seemed to interest all those present very deeply because already outside the Catholic Church there had been for some twenty years a very great desire to see the unity of Christendom on the part of all the Protestant bodies and some of the Orthodox ones. And the very fact of a contact, in those days, with the successor of St Peter was so unique an experience, that it really delighted them. Of course, it was a kind of forerunner of some of the things that were to happen later on. In these days one wouldn't think of any particular excitement being created by a remark that any non-Catholic had had an audience with the Pope. In the terms of Christian Unity, such events have become part of the international religious scene.

Whilst I speak of Canon Pass I must say that being present at that conference made me realise where the fullness of Christendom lay. Each morning, for several days, we went to the Old Catholic Church in Berne where the Canon celebrated the Eucharist. After a few days there, the Canon, feeling that the Old Catholics had become mainly an intellectual movement and had very little following, asked me to discover where the local Roman Catholic Church was. And after that we went each morning and simply attended Mass without any thought of going to Holy Communion, of course. In another way that old Canon said something that also brought me nearer to what I did in 1936 when I was received into the Church. I remember his saying that if he were Pope he would abolish the whole of the Old Testament and put Plato in its place. This seemed to me, even in those days, completely to overlook the fact that you cannot really understand the New Testament without the Old Testament, or the Old Testament without the New.

But I have not really answered your question. Over a number of years there were two friends of Oxford days who influenced my decision. Francis Head was at St Stephen's House, an Anglican theological college, then in Norham Gardens. I got to know him, I think, through Pusey House and we became close friends. He became a Catholic a number of years before I did and began his novitiate with the Jesuits. After his Oxford days we corresponded regularly. He had a very clear mind and wrote many letters, some of which I still have. He certainly helped to clear the path of my thinking and drew me on my pilgrim way. Ultimately he became a Catholic priest in the Diocese of Portsmouth and was killed in a motor accident. His mother had also been received into the Church and subsequently I took her to Rome. Francis was her only child and humanly speaking she was heartbroken and did not long survive him.

The other one who exercised an influence was Patrick Mclaughlin. He was a scholar of Worcester and we met in the OUDS as both of us were interested in theatricals and in acting. We also met often at the salon of Clara Harriet Browne and at Pusey House. He introduced me to the Dominicans at Blackfriars and together we attended lectures there on St Thomas Aquinas. His great interest in the Papal Encyclicals on social questions made me also realise their import. He was a year ahead of me and married on graduation. I was an usher at his wedding and became godfather to his first daughter. He made the way forward so clear to me that I expected him and his family to follow me when I was received some years later. But it took him another 25 years before he followed suit.

> *In 1968 you wrote an address to the clergy of the Diocese of Leeds in which you said that by the time you took your degree in 1932 you were "intellectually convinced of the Catholic position". Does this mean that you were already thinking about going a stage further and becoming a Roman Catholic?*

No, because at that time I don't think I had the gift of fullness of faith. In other words I wasn't ripe in 1932. At that time I knew so many people who thought as I did and were cleverer and indeed holier by far than I was, who held the same views but didn't see any reason to do anything about it. And I thought who am I to do it? Nonetheless even at that time - I think it must have been 1933 - a very unusual thing happened.

I was at an Anglican Theological College - St Stephen's House - and a friend of mine whose father was a Don at Christ Church came to me one day and said "My father has had an invitation from the Abbot of Buckfast to stay at the Abbey for a few days. Unfortunately my father can't go and he had been asked also to take me and any couple of my friends. There is a man from Oriel, Henry Lloyd, and an Austrian friend (he was the only Roman Catholic of the four). We would like you to join us as my father can't come. Would you like to come with us for a weekend to Buckfast?" I told him I'd love to go. So we went down by car and I can remember going into Salisbury Cathedral and Exeter Cathedral and finding them set out for concerts. I remember the Austrian who was with us saying as we entered these cathedrals, "Look at it, look at it, built for the Mass and look at it now turned into a concert hall!" and then we went on to Buckfast. Of course, I had read a lot about Monasteries and the Benedictine order and so forth, but it never occurred to me that this way of life was still going on in more or less pre-Reformation style. It was therefore an absolute revelation to be plunged into the Benedictine life of Buckfast Abbey. We were all swept off our feet. Moreover we had long talks with Abbot Vonier who, as you know was a great theologian and a deeply spiritual character. I can remember the three of us sitting up all night in the guest house at Buckfast, with the Austrian Catholic, wondering whether we ought to become Roman Catholics: and when we left Buckfast we wrote in the visitor's book *"QUIA VIDERUNT OCULI MEI SALUTARE TUUM":* "For mine eyes have seen thy salvation".

We went back to Oxford and all three of us went into the Dominican house, Blackfriars, and asked to be instructed and received into the Church. Looking back I can see that the Dominican priest realised that we had all been through a somewhat emotional experience at Buckfast; and anyhow the summer term was almost at an end. So he said to us: "Don't you think it would be much more realistic to be instructed in your own parishes?" As a result we went away to our different homes. I went and found the very lovely church, Our Lady of Ransom in Eastbourne, which was the nearest one to where my parents lived. There was a very nice priest there called Canon Walters. He was very understanding and I told him I wanted to be instructed. I didn't tell anyone else at this stage and I started instruction. After a few sessions I said to him "I am going to be in a very, very difficult position when I'm received into the church because my family think they have set me up as an Anglican clergyman, and they will think that now I'm throwing it all away. Isn't there any possibility of my getting accepted for priestly training in a Seminary?" He said "Well, it would be a most unusual request but I will speak to Bishop Amigo about it." To his surprise Bishop Amigo said he would see me and that he was going down to the church of the South African Fathers in Hastings. If I could go over there he would see me on a certain day. Well my mother used to like to go shopping in Hastings occasionally as well as in Eastbourne and so I said, "Will you come over to Hastings I'm going to see the Bishop of Southwark." This was very naughty of me, really, because there was an Anglican Bishop of Southwark as well as a Catholic Bishop of Southwark. Of course, she wasn't to know which one and so she said "Oh yes, you go and see the Bishop of Southwark, while I go and do some shopping, so we can have a pleasant afternoon." So I went to see Bishop Amigo and I was tremendously impressed by him because the only Bishops that I had met were Anglicans. But this venerable Bishop was to my mind much more the sort of man that Our Lord had chosen as His first Apostles. Despite his great learning and sanctity he was something of a rough diamond, from the Anglican point of view! This, I thought, is really "the fisherman of Galilee". I talked to him and he asked me some questions.

Eventually he said "Well, I'll tell you what you should do. You must go home and tell your parents what you are going to do and you will start going regularly to Mass and when you are received I will send you to teach at the John Fisher School at Purley for a couple of years and then if all goes well I will send you to a Seminary".

How did your family react to this development?

When I got home on that occasion my father alone was in the house. So I thought "Well I had better tell him that I have seen this Bishop and that I am under instruction and give him the reasons". And so I sat down to talk to him. I should tell you that my father was a very taciturn man; he rarely showed emotion of any kind and very rarely spoke. When he did, it was usually worth hearing. He listened to me as I rambled on and told him what had been in my mind for many years, how the whole thing had come to a crescendo, so to speak, and what I had been doing latterly in the way of being in touch with members of the Catholic Church. He didn't say anything and eventually I looked up at him; and for the first time in my life I saw tears trickling down his cheeks. That was a terrible shock to me. He then begged me not to go on with it. He said "This is far too great a step to take without much more consideration. You really must go back to your Anglican Theological College and you really must think about it much longer. I beg you not to tell your mother or anyone else at the moment because it will upset them terribly. So please will you think about it longer?" Well, I was devastated; but I went to see the Canon in Eastbourne who was instructing me and told him the situation. I said, "I am deeply sorry but really I cannot go on for the moment because this is going to upset not only my father but the whole family so terribly that I really will have to think about it very much longer. I am extremely sorry that this has only happened at this somewhat late stage; and I wonder if you will be so kind as to tell Bishop Amigo that I did as he asked me to do, but I just have not the courage at this moment to go ahead with it." The Canon was more than kind about it and very understanding. And so I went back to my Theological College.

I can remember I didn't unpack for two or three weeks. I was very unhappy and it could be thought that I was refusing a grace. Objectively I suppose I was. Subjectively maybe not. At any rate I was very upset and indeed I didn't really want to go forward to Anglican Ordination. I tried to fail the General Ordination Examination but I scraped through. And so it happened that I went to Chichester to be ordained Deacon by the then Bishop of Chichester, George Bell. He was a great and distinguished figure and an ecumenist ahead of his time. I was invited along with the other candidates who were to be ordained Deacon to stay at the Palace in Chichester where we had a kind of retreat. On that occasion there were other clergy also staying in the house and among them a certain Archdeacon. Each afternoon during the few days that we spent there, he took out different students for a long walk. I wondered what the purpose of this was until I was taken myself and accordingly discovered. On the walk he and I talked about trivialities for a short time. Then he suddenly stopped and he said "Now young man, I want you to give the first ten years of your life to God". I remember saying "Mr Archdeacon, I don't understand what you mean. If I am going to give myself to God at all, surely it ought to be a more generous gesture than that? Surely it ought to be something for the whole of one's life?" "Ah well, my dear boy, I think you misunderstood me. You see, I know you will see many pretty faces over the tennis net, but resist dear boy, resist. Don't get married for the first ten years." I really thought that this was a very extraordinary remark. But I had to go on with receiving the diaconate. All my family were coming to Chichester to stay there and so it took place. I then took up my curacy at St Bartholomew's, Brighton and the Vicar there was a certain T. Dilworth Harrison, who three or four months later was appointed Archdeacon of Chesterfield, in Derbyshire.

When a person is ordained in the Church of England he has to get an incumbent of a parish to accept him as his assistant. Then the Bishop of that Diocese is the one that ordains him in the first place deacon and subsequently priest. I had met Dilworth Harrison when he gave a mission in Oxford. He was a fine pastoral man and when he invited me to go as his assistant, I said "Yes". So, as I was saying, when he was appointed to Chesterfield, and further asked me to go with him there, it was a very unusual thing to happen for somebody who was still only a deacon. It would mean that if I went I would have to be ordained priest by the Bishop of Derby and that would imply that I must get the guidance of the Bishop of Chichester as to what I should do. So I went to see him and I told him of the situation and he said "Yes, well if you ask me what you should do, I think you should go with him because I don't know anyone who is a finer instructor of young clergy." So I said "Thank you very much" and, of course, I went with him.

Did your own position regarding Roman Catholicism have any effect on your work as an Anglican curate during this period?

In one particular instance it certainly did. While I was a young curate at this church of St Bartholomew in Brighton a woman came and told me of her difficulties about the whole question of whether or not she ought to be a Catholic. I listened to her and put forward what defence I could give for the Church of England. But after several sessions she went on pursuing the matter and eventually I said "Look here, if you really see things as clearly as that you had better talk to a Catholic priest because I share so many of your views and if I saw the situation as clearly as you do I would go and become a Catholic tomorrow". "Thank you," she said "that's all I want to know. Would you be so kind as to come to the station and see me on the train to Bath, because I shall go to Downside Abbey where I have a friend called Dom Christopher Butler who has just become a monk there." He was also a convert clergyman from the Church of England. She had known him as a Chaplain at Brighton College.

I went and saw her off and then called in at St Bartholomew's Church. An order of Anglican nuns worked in the parish and as I went into the church strangely enough the Reverend Mother of the Order came up to me. "Oh brother," she said "I do hope that you will do everything you can to stop Mrs X. from becoming a Catholic" "Well sister," I said, "I really must tell you straight away that I have been discussing this problem with her for some time and I came to the conclusion that the only solution for her is to become a Roman Catholic. So she has already gone on her way to Rome and I have just been to see her off to Downside Abbey." She was terribly angry and she rushed into the vestry where the Vicar was and I could hear an awful row going on behind the doors. She was shouting "You and I have been keeping this woman back for I don't know how many years and this wretched young curate comes along and in a month or two has done all this damage." So I thought "Oh dear, well I'd better go back to the clergy house and see what he is going to say to me." He didn't say anything that day and he didn't say anything the next day and I thought "Well this can't go on." So after that I went and knocked at his door and said "May I come in?" He said "Yes". I said "I think you must know what I have done with regard to this person who wanted to become a Catholic." And he said "Well yes, sit down and I'll tell you now. I can understand in a sense what you did, though of course you shouldn't have done it. Nevertheless," he said, "I do understand because for the first ten years of my own ordination in the Church of England my first thought every morning and my last every night was ought I to become a Roman Catholic?" So I said to him "What did you do about it?" He said "I regarded it as a temptation severely to be resisted and after ten years it disappeared." I then said "That might have been a refusal of grace". And of course he didn't like that. "No." he said, "Now you must study anew the Epistles of St Paul because you will find that the primitive church was something very, very different from what the Roman Catholic church is today." So I really did start studying the Epistles of St Paul but the more I read of them the more it seemed to me that he was describing the very church that I wanted to join and was certainly not describing the Church of England with all its dissensions and differences. Moreover the Vicar had said to me in the course of our conversation "I will tell you now that there is one book I never dare read again" and I said "What is that?" He hedged about it for some time, then he said "Well it is a book called *The Price of Unity* by Father Maturin" He was a Cowley father who became a Catholic. So I said "Will you lend it to me?" He said "Oh" and passed it off and gave me the impression that he hadn't got it. A few days later he was ill in bed and he asked me to go down to his study and get a certain book for him and there right next door to the book on the shelf was *The Price of Unity* by Father Maturin. So I took it and read it and yes it helped me on. Soon after this the time came for us to go to Chesterfield and there I was very happy, humanly speaking, happier than I was in Brighton, because I loved Derbyshire, and its people and felt very much at home.

Dilworth Harrison himself was a man for whom one could only have a very great regard because he was a very pastoral person, a very dedicated person. He was a celibate and he was very well known throughout the country as a preacher. But there were some harder sides to his regime. For example, none of his curates was allowed to smoke until after lunch. Lunch was always followed by a cup of coffee and then the Archdeacon would rise and say "Well now this is neither fishing nor mending nets, let us go about our business. Door to door visitation. And don't have any cups of tea and be back in the parish church for Evensong at six o'clock." This was complicated by the fact that we had to hand in every Monday morning a form in which we recounted all the visits and other pastoral things that we had done in the previous week. Every Monday morning there was a review of these forms. We had to pass these time sheets to the Archdeacon and he went through each one and commented on it, asking questions about the various things.

I had a fellow curate there who was a very dear and a very amusing person, with a great sense of humour, but he had a thyroid problem and he used to get very exhausted and when he was sent out on his house to house visiting in the afternoon, he quite often fell asleep in various houses. So much so that I heard one old lady in Chesterfield say to another "What do you do, love, when he falls asleep in the house." She said "Oh, I just wake him up later on with a cup of tea." Anyway he found this a very great strain. About that time I had been given, by my grandfather, my first car, a small Morris Cowley with a dickey seat. So when we went out to start our visiting he would say to me "I really can't go visiting this afternoon, can't you take me up in your car onto the Derbyshire Moors." I was only too glad to have such an excuse. And so off we went. Half way along he would begin to get scruples and say "I really don't know what I am going to put on my time sheet." And I said "That's over to you to decide what you are going to put." And then I saw him take out a piece of paper from his pocket, and a pen, and every time we came to a signpost, pointing to different places, he copied the name down and the following Monday morning his time sheet would read as follows: such and such an afternoon - visited Mrs Matlock, Mrs Baslow, Mr Spitewinter and various other names of the Derbyshire areas through which we had passed. All sorts of different names. Well I nearly broke down, as you can imagine, in the post mortem because he was then closely questioned about these people that the Archdeacon, himself, had never come across. He wanted to know where they lived and more about them. I think it taught him and me a lesson: "Oh, what a tangled web we weave when first we labour to deceive."

On other occasions the Archdeacon was in great demand as a preacher and we sometimes had to stand in for him. I can remember having to stand in for him on a course on the History of the Church of England. He dictated to me what I was to say in the lecture for which he couldn't be present himself, and as he did so I said "But that isn't true, that just isn't true." He said "Well, I think you had better say it just the same" and so I found myself in a very, very difficult situation. It was another of those matters that led me on to trying to follow Newman's message inscribed on his tomb: "Ex umbris et imaginibus in veritatem".

It was while I was at Chesterfield that I was ordained in Derby Cathedral. Before that however I had gone and had a retreat and tried to sort things out and found some help in the advice of the then vicar of All Saints, Margaret Street, who was an Anglican Benedictine. He was very sympathetic about the situation but tried to reassure me that I was doing the right thing in going forward as a priest in the Church of England. So it went off all right but I was still in my heart unhappy about things. After a year or so I developed jaundice and I was taken into a nursing home because they wanted to try and find out the cause of it. Looking back I think the cause of it was really the strain of this question that had been going on for four years and to which I hadn't really faced up. The doctor (who didn't know about this) said "I think you perhaps need to return to the southern climate". It so happened at that time that I was offered two things: one was to be a curate at St Giles', Cambridge which appealed to me because I was interested in doing some further study; also I was asked if I would go as an assistant chaplain to Lancing College the big Woodard school on the South Coast. The Anglican clergy who advised me and were friends from Oxford days urged me to go to Lancing because there was a new Headmaster there and he badly needed a sort of Anglo-Catholic input into the life of the school which had fallen away from those sort of ideas to some extent. And so to Lancing I went and there humanly speaking I was very happy. But it was only for a relatively short time because in teaching religion throughout the school, the picture became clearer and clearer to me about what I must do. I also think that when I was at Lancing, with the responsibility of teaching all these boys, I prayed more than I had ever done before.

Much as I liked being at Lancing I don't really think I was very much good as a school master. In fact, what I am about to relate portrays a regrettable example on my part in which the boy concerned certainly got the better of me. The class were writing an essay on something or other and I was just walking round the room, seeing how they were getting on when I came to a boy to whom, a short time previously, I had given a small punishment for some misdemeanour. In those days it was all done by imposing lines, and I had given him twenty lines. As he was writing his essay I found one of his pockets was bulging and I said "What have you got in that pocket?" He said "A packet of crisps, Sir." "Oh," I said, "I like those. If you like to hand them over I will let you off those twenty lines." And hand them over he did. Later that day I had to give a further punishment to another boy who had committed a worse misdemeanour and he was given a hundred lines. Next day I said as they came into class "Have you done those hundred lines I gave you?" He said "No sir, but here are five packets of potato crisps"!

How did it come about that during your time at Lancing you finally decided to become a Roman Catholic?

I had a great friend there, a house-master called Patrick Halsey with whom I always kept in-touch; we were very close friends until his death quite recently. We went on many continental tours together and he and I went on the Grand Tour of Italy in the summer of 1936. It was in Rome that things came to a head for me. We had an audience out at Castelgandolfo with Pope Pius XI. It made a very great impression on me. His motto was *Fides Intrepida* - "Intrepid Faith". He had been the Librarian of the Ambrosian Library in Milan, an Alpine climber, and was a very strong personality. Although it was a general audience it had a great impact on me and I felt in Rome itself that I really must talk to a Catholic priest again, but I didn't know anybody. I did know, however, that there was an English College in Rome and I knew there must be a Rector. So I wrote to him and asked him if I could see him. I was staying in a hotel, the Savoia in the Via Ludovisi off the Veneto, and days passed and there was no answer. On the morning that I was leaving with my friends to go to Naples I got a telephone call in this hotel from the Rector of the English College saying "I'm so sorry, I have only today received your letter because I have been out at the Villa at Palazzola and I have just returned. If I can be of any help to you, would you like me to come along there?" and I said "Yes, that's very kind of you. I have got to go on the one o'clock train to Naples but if you are able to come I will be very pleased to see you." So he came and it was by talking to him for an hour or more that it became absolutely clear to me what I should do. I remember sitting up all night in Parker's Hotel in Naples writing my letters of resignation. And then I had the long journey home without being able to tell anybody, even my closest friends, what I had done. Then I had to face all over again the breaking of the news to the family.

That conversation in Rome with Monsignor Godfrey, as he then was, provided the final clarification, so to speak, of the situation. I had been agonising for a good four years and I knew now that whatever the cost, I had to face up to it. But I would say that in our talk he gave me clear guidance as to what I should do. I told him what I held and what had happened so far and he said "Well when you have got the gift of the fullness of the Faith, you should take it with both hands because it is always very dangerous to refuse to accept it: for it is God-given". He also said "Remember what the Gospel says, and what Our Lord says that 'if any man love father, mother, brother, sister, etc more than me, he is not worthy of me'" and that struck me very deeply.

Before I could return home to England there was a long continuation of the Italian tour. We went on to Venice and the Italian lakes, but really I went on in a sort of daze. I remember my father meeting me at Newhaven and from there he drove me to our lovely home in Sussex. I didn't say anything to him, I thought this time I would speak to my mother about it to begin with and so that I did. We went on a country walk together and I broke the news to her. Of course, she was very upset and so much so that I almost had to carry her home. But she quickly recovered and when she saw that I was absolutely determined to do something about it, she said she thought I should go off to Downside Abbey and it would be better if I left it to her to tell my father and my sister. I was grateful for not having to face my father again at that stage. I went off to Downside and started my instructions. I went to Downside because the lady who had gone from Brighton and been received into the church had told the monks about me and they had extended an open invitation to me. She herself had been received into the Church and was living in the village of Downside. She gave me an introduction to Dom Christopher Butler and it was arranged that I should go there. This appealed to me very much because I already knew some of the Downside monks from the Lancing days. In those days what is now the big Catholic public school of Worth, in Sussex, was then a prep school for Downside and I used sometimes to go over there from Lancing.

Whilst I was at Downside I received a telegram from my family asking me to return home. When I got that telegram I found it very difficult to decide what I should do and so I asked to see the Abbot of Downside, Dom Bruno Hicks. He had been very kind to me already, and I asked him what I should do. He said "You must go." I said "But Father Abbot, four years ago I reached this stage and I didn't have the courage to go on with being received and I am afraid that exactly the same thing will happen again, given human weakness," "It will not happen again" he said "We shall all be sustaining you by our prayers and you must go." So I did go and I was wonderfully sustained by their prayers on that journey. When I got home my mother said how sorry she was that the telegram had been sent and she also gave me great consolation by saying that although she didn't understand in the least what I was doing, she felt a secret joy in her heart about it. She also said "You will I hope go on to be a priest" and I said "Well now that is something that remains to be seen because the Catholic priesthood is something very different from the Anglican ministry, due to celibacy and all sorts of other reasons." "Well" she said "the one thing that I'm absolutely sure about is that God wants you to be a priest."

I then had a very difficult weekend of non-stop talks with my father. This was all the more difficult because there were a lot of visitors staying with us at the time. I remember sitting in a twin bedroom, me on one bed and he on the other and hammering and hammering this out, but we never got any further and eventually my mother said "Look this is doing no good to either of you. It is time that you went back". So I did go back and resumed my instructions and was received into the Church in the Lady Chapel at Downside on September 18th. The two witnesses were Dom Christopher Butler, who later became Bishop Butler and before that had become Abbot of Downside, and Dom Oswald Sumner; also present was the lady from Brighton.

It is with great affection that I recall them all, especially dear old Father Richard Davey, who later became the titular Abbot of Glastonbury, and who had instructed me and received me. This outcome was a great joy and a great relief. But then, of course, the question immediately arose as to what I should do. I would like to have gone straight into the monastery at Downside but in those days they wouldn't allow one to do that sort of thing. It was necessary to go away for two or three years and do something in a more ordinary manner, before you could be regarded as sufficiently settled and mature as a Catholic to go into the monastery.

Nevertheless a very wonderful thing happened. On the same day that I was received who should turn up at Downside but Monsignor Charles Duchemin who was the Rector of the Beda College in Rome. He was an old boy of the school at Downside and had come there to celebrate his 50th birthday on that very day. I was introduced to him and we had a long talk. He said that he had a long waiting list at the college but that if I could get a Bishop to take me on, he had just had one unexpected cancellation and he would give the place to me and take me there straight away. I heard at the same time from a friend of mine called Nora Wallis, whom I'd known for many years through Oxford friends. She had been received into the church some time previously and intimated that if I was going forward to the priesthood she would like to sponsor me financially at a seminary, on the understanding I would go to the Diocese of Westminster. So I approached Dr Hinsley, then Archbishop of Westminster, and I had a very pleasant interview with him. I told him quite frankly that I really thought that I wanted to be a Benedictine and not a secular priest. "Well" he said "don't worry about that. I will sponsor you to go to the Beda as Monsignor Duchemin has requested. As Miss Wallis is financing you and as you're not costing the Diocese anything, if you ever do want to go to Downside you will be free to do so."

There is one other incident that I would like to tell you about. Like so many school masters in those days, I used to do all my foreign travel on an overdraft in anticipation of my next payment of salary and so by September 1936 I was fifty pounds overdrawn in my personal account and I did not know how I could meet it. I was talking to one of the monks about it. He said "You ask St Therese of Lisieux to do something about that for you. She is very good on those sort of things." So I did and a few days later I received a letter with a French stamp and the postmark of Lisieux on it, and inside was a cheque for £50. Now I hadn't asked anybody for that but it so happened that a friend who was staying at Lisieux had decided that I might be short of money and had sent me this. It all seemed to be very much in the hands of God's providence. Very soon afterwards my father, who had told me when I left home that I wasn't to return, was persuaded by an uncle of mine that such a barrier shouldn't exist between father and son, whatever had happened. Thus, I was able to go home and our relationship ultimately became very close again. It remained so throughout the next 35 years until he died in November 1971. It was a great joy to me when he came to St Anne's Cathedral in 1966 when I was enthroned as Bishop of Leeds.

Why do you think your father was so opposed to your decision to become a Roman Catholic?

Well in those days you know there were no grants for people to go to university. If you went to Oxford as a Commoner, which I did in the first instance before I got that small exhibition from the college, you had to be sponsored by your parents. This was always to some extent a sacrifice for them. They made it very willingly for me because they felt that they wanted to ensure my future by giving me a very complete education, which wasn't everybody's lot in those days. I suppose they thought that I was throwing away all the opportunities they had made possible for me, which is understandable.

Was there any reaction to what had happened from people at Lancing College?

The whole experience was a very traumatic one given the attitudes which prevailed at that time, and thank God the lights of ecumenism have made these situations generally speaking - though not always - much easier for people today. I can remember one other person from the school who became a Catholic whose father asked him to change his name by deed poll when he took that step. For my part I promised to say as little about the matter as possible because the Headmaster and everybody had been very kind to me but they were afraid that parents would remove their boys from the school where so pernicious an influence had been at work. Some time afterwards, however, I remember meeting one of the boys I had taught at Lancing. This boy came up to me and said "Oh, hello, Sir, what's happened to you? Why haven't you come back to us this term?" So I said, "Well, don't you know?" He said "The boys do say, Sir, that you've run off with a barmaid." "Well," I said, "I don't think she's generally called a barmaid, but I have heard her referred to as a scarlet woman."

After all these years how do you look back on these events in 1936?

Perhaps I could answer this question by telling you of an incident which took place a few years ago. In 1976 I had the joy of being present at the installation of Basil Hume as Archbishop of Westminster. After the ceremony in the Cathedral many of us went on to Westminster Abbey with the Cardinal to hear the Benedictine monks sing in the Abbey just as they did four hundred years ago. This was one of the highlights of a memorable day and a very moving occasion. Afterwards an Anglican clergyman came up to me and said "I imagine that if this had happened forty years ago you would never have left us." I had to think for a moment, and I had to be charitable, and I said something like this: "I should be very sorry indeed if it had stopped me." Because the joy of being a Catholic has always far outweighed the sorrows, trials and even the changes that one has had to endure. After all, the gift of the fullness of the Faith is the greatest gift - and I believe this with all my heart - that God can give to any man or woman in this life.

THE YEARS OF PRIESTHOOD

One thing that become apparent from looking back on your early life is the fact that both as an Anglican and a Roman Catholic you wanted to be a priest. At what age did you first sense that you had such a vocation?

I am not sure whether it was in 1916 or 1917 that I was taken to stay with an Uncle who lived in York. I remember that childhood visit very vividly and in subsequent years when I was asked at what age I first wanted to be a clergyman I would give the reply that this desire began in York Minster on an Easter Sunday when I was 6 or 7 years old. Resurrection had something to do with it. And later on I linked it with the shrine of St William of York. That beloved Minster had a new significance for me subsequently because it was within the territory of the Catholic diocese in which I first became a Bishop.

Doubtless many people have had a childhood experience of this kind which has perhaps persisted. It certainly did with me and I never thought very seriously of ever becoming anything other than a cleric. That was my main reason for going to Oxford although I chose to read History before moving on to Theology.

When I became a Catholic, I hesitated initially regarding going on to the Priesthood. There was the question of celibacy which was not required of an Anglican cleric. There was also the necessity in those days of spending at least four more years of study before ordination as a Priest. Did I feel, as many of my contemporaries did, that I was a Priest already? It seemed quite clear to me that I did not think of myself as a Priest in the Roman Catholic sense. I can remember the very day when I knew that I could never again celebrate the Anglican Eucharist. But the desire and longing for a priestly life persisted. After my reception into the Church circumstances seemed to decree in a quite remarkable way that I should go straight ahead. And for that grace I have ever been full of gratitude. A priestly vocation is a Divine Call as well as an offering of one's inadequate self.

You have touched here on the question of the validity

of Anglican orders. There are people on both sides who seem anxious to initiate a new approach to this matter. Would you agree with that?

As we know in 1896, Pope Leo XIII, after 4 years of preliminary discussions in which Anglicans played a part, issued the Bull *APOSTOLICAE CURAE*, declaring Anglican ordinations to be invalid from the Catholic viewpoint; having defect of Form and Intention. The practice of the Catholic Church regarding convert clergy from the 16th Century onwards had invariably been that of ordaining them to the priesthood absolutely. And this practice is still continued. It has been thought, however, by some that the situation has now been changed by the official participation of Dutch Old Catholic bishops (whose Orders are recognised by Rome) in a number of Anglican ordinations, as well as an unofficial infiltration from some Eastern Orthodox prelates. The whole question of ministry has been discussed in the ARCIC dialogue and the desirability expressed of an approach to mutual recognition. To my mind this approach should not in any way affect the verdict of Leo XIII which from the Catholic viewpoint was absolutely justified in 1896. Indeed, to my mind it could still be absolutely justified to-day since it would be extremely difficult to pin-point the extent of any infiltration of validity. Therefore any truly ecclesial unity will best be served by an approach which calls for a new validation from the Catholic viewpoint and which assuredly in dialogue could be achieved. As I speak, however, the obex of women bishops and priests, as well as other contradictions regarding matters of Faith and Morals, is likely to defer any growth of unity in the foreseeable future. This is a cause of great sadness on both sides for many people who long to embark upon a joint new re-evangelisation of our country. For this to be effective there must be a united front. Let us pray God Our Father to bring it about despite our failure as He alone can.

Looking back to 1936 can you explain the reason why you left the Church of England and became a Roman Catholic? Was it the case that you were repelled by Anglicanism or was it more a case of being attracted by Roman Catholicism?

I don't, of course, like the word "repelled" because I thank God for the training that He gave me in faith in the Anglican

Church. I must admit that I was repelled by the idiosyncrasies that I found and the uncertainties regarding fundamental things. With regard to the Roman Catholic Church, yes there was a special attraction in those days, regarding liturgy but also regarding Unity, Holiness, Apostolicity, Universality, and Authority. Fundamentally the call to me was to be one with the Universal Church. I had never really thought of the Anglican Church as a Universal Church in the sense that the Catholic Church is. Nor have I ever regarded any authority in the Church of England as measuring up to that authority which Our Lord gave to St Peter and consequently to his successors.

> *So the two key issues here are the Universality of the Roman Catholic Church and the authority, God-given, of the Papacy?*

Yes. I have never for a moment had any regret regarding these fundamental issues. I can remember six months after I had been received into the Catholic Church, an Anglican Bishop wrote a letter to my mother in which he said "I understand that people who have become Roman Catholics have a sort of reaction. I would like you to know that if your son is going through a phase of this kind I would want to do everything possible to welcome him back." I never knew about this until later because I had never gone through that phase, thank God. Everyone in the Catholic Church had been so wonderfully kind and helpful. But my mother quite unbeknown to me, at the time, wrote back to the Bishop a quite indignant letter saying she knew her son and his mind better than that and there was no thought of any such thing. He was extremely happy, she said, at his college in Rome and was making progress towards the Catholic priesthood.

> *Your reception into the Catholic Church in September 1936 was quickly followed by your departure for Rome and the Beda College where you were to study for the priesthood. What does your time in Rome mean to you now, half a century later?*

I still count my time at the Beda as one of the greatest things in my life. It was marvellous to get to Rome away from all the insularity of our own country and to be in the centre of the Universal Church. It became a wonderful experience which I look back upon with great thanksgiving.

In those days, the Beda College was in the Via San Nicolo da Tolentino, which was off the Piazza Barberini, very much in the centre of Rome. It was a lovely situation from that point of view. The building had originally been a hotel and later a convent before the Beda College moved in. So internally it had a rather run-down appearance. There was, for example, a lift shaft but no lift. I was assigned a room up 150 steps and it overlooked a *Cortile* on the opposite side of which were residential flats. At times it could be very noisy. Three sides of it were the Beda and the fourth side, although it had been purchased by the College, was never incorporated into the main building. I had been living in some very pleasant surroundings at Lancing, as you can imagine, and my Roman apartment was very different: a stone floor, an iron bedstead, and an enamel wash-basin on an iron tripod. There was one chest of drawers that was practically eaten away by wood-worm and it looked as though it might collapse at any moment. Of course, I was ready for anything at 26 and although it was not very attractive I thought that sooner or later I would get used to it. On my arrival, however, I decided to try and forget it for the moment and so I went to bed. As soon as I lay on the bed, the two ends of the bed met over the top of me and the whole thing collapsed on to the floor and that made me laugh. It broke the ice, so to speak, and I never looked back. In fact, I became very fond of that little cell and later on, of course, I did graduate to a very much nicer room.

There was a wonderful spirit in the college. It has been described as a cross between a senior common room and an officers' mess because there were late vocations of all kinds there and the average age of the students was very much higher than my then age. I was one of the youngest people there. It was a lovely experience to be in that community. There were about 75 or 80 of them I suppose, from a wide variety of backgrounds. To know them became a most enriching experience. There were so many people from all parts of the world. They weren't only from England, Ireland and Scotland, they were also from America, from Canada and from India and all sorts of far-flung English speaking countries: Australians, New Zealanders and so forth. It was a very deeply interesting experience. Spiritually, I was radiantly happy and I never looked back from that point of view, by God's grace. There was a lovely chapel there, a pleasant common room, and the food was excellent. We couldn't afford things like butter but apart from that it was very good. This was the height of the fascist regime and there were great sufferings. I can remember at one stage Italy ran out of coffee beans. Quite suddenly, however, they sold a footballer to the Argentines and asked them to pay for him with vast quantities of coffee beans. And so for a short time after that we had the most delicious coffee. It didn't last for very long and subsequently we returned to ground acorns. By and large, we were well looked-after. The pasta and the vino alike were excellent. We enjoyed too the friendship of the Italian people, despite the international situation in the late thirties. It was very sad that they were driven into the arms of Hitler over the Abyssinian war and with hindsight our pre-war diplomats might have handled things better. Whilst I was there Hitler came to Rome and I remember seeing him as I walked through the Borghese Gardens. He was in a car with a great escort and accompanied by Goering and Goebbels and all those people. The streets of Rome were hung with swastikas and I always recall Pope Pius XI saying "There is a cross today in the streets of Rome which is not the Cross of Christ". By this time he had no illusions regarding Hitler and indeed in 1937 he wrote the famous encyclical, *Mit brennender Sorge,* which denounced Nazism. It was a very fascinating time, as you can imagine, to be there.

I shall never forget my first private audience with Pope Pius XI. My memory of him will always be of a man of deep and solid and intrepid faith. I remember being taken by Archbishop Hinsley, as one of his Westminster students, (there were about 7 or 8 of us) into the private study of the Pope. As we entered it was in those days the custom to make three genuflections as for royalty, and then kiss the Fisherman's ring and the foot of the Pontiff. So it was a very extraordinary experience for me. An amusing thing happened because Arthur Hinsley's Italian had its limitations. When he introduced to the Pope two others and myself who were formerly Anglican clergy, the Italian words conveyed that we were "antique" Anglican clerics. It was the only time I saw Pius XI laugh. We were in Rome when Chamberlain came with Halifax to try to counteract the Berlin-Rome Axis which alas was to lead to the Second World War. The Italian people as such were much more on our side but, of course, the Fascists had to be on the side of the Germans. I remember a question in Rome at the time: "Why are there three cordons of the Italian Army drawn up round the Trevi fountain?" (into which people throw their coins to make sure they come back). The answer was "To stop Hitler from throwing his coins into it".

Whilst I was a student in Rome the saddest thing of my life happened: the final illness and early death of my mother in January 1938. Hinsley was very kind and I was given permission to go home to her, which was an unusual concession in those days, and to stay with her as long as she needed me. I was with her for some months and this was a great consolation for she was dying of cancer. She was only fifty seven when she died. My father lived to be ninety two and yet in those days one could never have thought of his being left without her. It was a great shock to all of us and it was a very difficult time. We were miles away from a Catholic church, but they used to lend me the car every morning to go to Mass at 7 o'clock, 4 or 5 miles away and that too was a great consolation. My mother wanted me to tell her all about the Catholic Faith. If I had been a priest then I would have received her into the Church. But she sank lower and lower and lower, poor soul, as she couldn't swallow or digest any food. She took her sufferings completely in her stride. She had a little crucifix that had come from Jerusalem opposite her bed and I remember saying to her "Is there anything I can get for you now, or anything I can do for you?" and she said "No. All I want now is that." And she pointed to the crucifix. So it was she died, God rest her, in the early weeks of 1938. But in the meantime I had to go back to Rome when the new academic year began. I'd done some of the Philosophy studies whilst I was at home and in view of that they let me go straight onto Theology when I got back for the Autumn term. So I was in Rome when she died and unable to attend her funeral at Westham in Sussex, such was the expense and time needed to travel from Rome to England in those days; it was fully understood. So it wasn't until the summer of 1938 that I saw her grave when I went home. Our home was given up. My father left it when my sister married, and eventually lived most happily with her and her husband for all his remaining years.

My mother's death was a great blow to me because she had been so wonderful about my becoming a Catholic, especially when she urged me to become a priest. It was an extraordinary thing for her to do, as there was a belief amongst some of my relations that as I was an only son I should think of carrying on the family name.

I was in Rome until the summer of 1939 when we came home for the long vacation. During that vacation the war broke out and it was then that the Beda College was evacuated to a wing of St Joseph's College, Upholland in Lancashire. It was a very different setting. There was a sort of bathos in changing your address from Rome to Wigan! I was only there for a year but I count it as a very enriching year because it was an enormous help to me in later years to realise the sort of seminary life that the younger students had gone through. But you see we were still the Beda College and a separate entity when we went to Upholland. Of course we were regarded as rather "lax" compared with their rule. Dr Garvin who was a great wit in the Liverpool Diocese made a speech some years afterwards on the history of St Joseph's College and said "In 1939 the Beda College, in view of the war was evacuated from Rome to a wing of the college in Upholland. That was Upholland's first taste of the permissive society". Well it wasn't like that really. It was a very enriching experience and one made many new friends with the students of Upholland.

By the time we went to Upholland most of our studies had been completed and I always look back on the training provided at the Beda with deep gratitude. All the lectures took place in the college. The reason for that was because when the Beda college was founded (and it was to be a shorter period of studies for convert clergymen and mature people: four years instead of seven) it was thought better to do all the lectures in the vernacular so that the men didn't have to get used to Roman Latin. In the Roman universities all the lectures in those days were in Latin and it was the 'lingua franca'. Students at the English College will tell you that it took them about 6 months to get their ears tuned in to what was being said and after that they were all right. I used to go to some other lectures and of course when I was in the Second Vatican Council I had to listen to all the interventions in Latin. I even had to deliver speeches in Latin. It was a help that I had done classical studies until I specialised in history and so it didn't worry me very much especially as it was a very Italianate, medieval form of Latin. Some of my Anglican friends said that at the Beda I would be receiving a sort of 'peptonised' instruction. But it wasn't like that at all. The finest theological professor I ever encountered was the resident professor at the Beda: a Dutchman called Dr Schutt. He was one of those tremendous academic people who spent eight hours each day preparing his lectures and bringing them to life and I was more enriched by his lectures in dogmatic theology than by anything I had done in the whole of my course in Oxford. The Beda course was magnificent and I never in subsequent years felt at a loss academically. Dr Schutt died in Rome, and we missed him greatly in England.

As you have said, Rome in the late 1930s was in many ways a different world from the one you had lived in previously; you must have made many friends during that period of your life?

Indeed, in the college I made some very lasting friendships. First of all with the Rector himself Monsignor Duchemin who became a very devoted friend of mine and when he died I preached his panegyric. He was a very wonderful person, and I have great gratitude for having met him. When I first went to the Beda I found a number of Oxford acquaintances who became close friends: George Arthur Tomlinson, Roscoe Beddoes, Ken Oliver Carter, Bryan Houghton, and others. Then there was Tim McCarthy who remained a life-long friend and benefactor. In addition, a lot of the students became very close friends of mine until their death and there are still some alive, with whom I'm in touch, contemporaries of mine, but not many now. There were great influences there. Another thing: in those days the Beda was so central in Rome that any Englishman who came to stay in Rome, on the grand tour or anything else, was received at the Beda. There was great hospitality at the high table and one met all the leading figures in English Catholicism, all the Bishops of the country, all the leading laymen. It was a very interesting experience. I have always felt that Rome for me was the perfect completion of Oxford.

There are, however, two friends in particular who come to mind from these years, albeit for different reasons. The first was a man from Ireland, a much older man than I was then, whom I first met in the refectory of the Beda College. By the time I arrived there in 1936 he was well on with his studies but subsequently a very close friendship arose between us. His story is a very moving one to my mind, and I had a very great regard for him. In his younger days he had inherited a family shop and he had long decided that when he had saved up enough money from this business to pay for his own training to the priesthood he would try to find a Bishop who would accept him and send him to the college in Rome. At last the day came when he was putting up the shutters and the shop was to be closed. An old friend of his came to bid him farewell, a man who had a very high reputation as a devoted layman and who was also a man of considerable intelligence. They discussed what was going to happen and his friend said "Well Michael, I do so envy you because all my life I have wanted to offer myself for the priesthood in the same sort of way as you are doing. But I have never been in a position to finance my own studies and it is unfair at our age to put the cost of our training on a diocese." To which Michael replied. "Patrick, you are a far better man than I am. I am going to hand over to you the amount that I have saved and I want you please to take it and to go to the college if you can get a bishop to accept you. And if this can be done, I will at once take down the shutters and open the shop again." This took place, but about six months later when the other man had already been accepted and sent to the college, Michael won a very large sum of money in the Irish Sweep which meant that his generosity had given the Lord two priests instead of one. I was always very deeply touched by this. When he was ordained priest and was going back to work in Ireland he said to me, to my surprise "Now I am going to tell you something. You are the only Englishman I have ever liked and I am sure you have got some Irish blood in you somewhere!"

Another friendship made at the Beda College resulted in a very interesting experience for me as a young man living in Rome at an historic time. It happened in a very extraordinary way. I was asked by a friend of mine, Father Walter Meyjes, if I would serve his first Mass when he was ordained priest. When this took place I went down to the Church where the event was to happen. It was the Church of Santa Andrea delle Fratte in Rome. When I got there I found a great canopy outside and a red carpet running all down the nave and towards the chapel on the left hand side, which was a famous shrine of Our Lady. There in the Sanctuary was a gold chair and to my surprise seated in the gold chair was a figure that I recognised as the exiled King of Spain, Alphonso XIII. In those days, when a Sovereign was in the Sanctuary for Mass, the server took the Book of the Gospels for him to kiss after the Gospel had been read.

Later on I went out to have breakfast with the new priest and I said "I am surprised you didn't tell me that Alphonso XIII was going to be present in the Sanctuary, how does that come about?" "Oh," he said "my parents used to spend the winter in a hotel in Lausanne in Switzerland and I used to go and stay with them there and I was very interested in table tennis. The King of Spain was staying there as well and he also was a keen table tennis player and we found that we matched one another extremely well and a close friendship developed. He was very interested to hear that I was studying for the priesthood and he eventually said to me "When you are a priest I shall hope to come to your first Mass and give you a gold chalice"". The gold chalice had been given and used at the first Mass. Father Meyjes then said to me "I hope you are free at lunchtime because the King has invited us to lunch in the Royal Suite in the Grand Hotel, where he has been living since his exile." You can imagine my surprise, therefore, when as a young student I found myself as a guest of the exiled King of Spain.

We went to his apartments and were received with great kindness. Alphonso XIII suffered from the haemophilia of the Bourbon-Hapsburgs and he wore all the time grey suede mittens. I can picture him now pouring out the sherry himself in his own masked hands. He entertained us right royally with a champagne lunch, and there were a number of other interesting people there. Afterwards we went into his study with him where he had round the walls maps showing the advance of Franco's forces and he predicted almost to the week when the civil war in Spain would end. It was a fascinating experience for a young student as you can imagine.

There was a very nice sequel to it subsequently, only a few years ago, when I was in Spain visiting the English College in Valladolid. It had been arranged that while I was in Spain I would travel to Madrid with Mgr Ryan the then Rector, for an audience with King Juan Carlos as the King was anxious to have some conversation with an English Bishop regarding education in the Catholic public schools. Afterwards I told the King that I had known his Grandfather. He was extremely interested in this because as he said to me "That is more than I can say because I was only born in the city of Rome about the time that you are describing and my grandfather died before I became old enough to know him." This seemed to me a very interesting co-incidence and one that was a memorable occasion also.

Following the completion of your studies for the priesthood your ordination took place in the early months of the Second World War. What were the circumstances surrounding your ordination?

It took place in the crypt of Westminster Cathedral on 31st March 1940. The reason for it being held in the crypt was the war, of course. The Cathedral was all heavily sandbagged and it was thought that any ceremony that was likely to be a long one should be held down below rather than above ground. And so that is how I came to be ordained by Cardinal Hinsley, the Archbishop of Westminster, along with a number of my contemporaries from the Beda in the crypt. My Aunt Ida came. She had become a Catholic. My sister, Betty, and her husband, Jack Easton, also came and in the years since we have constantly had a very close relationship. Afterwards we went on to Norfolk in a blacked out train, so that I could say my first Mass in the Slipper Chapel at Walsingham.

By coincidence the Apostolic Delegate, Cardinal Godfrey, was in Walsingham at the time. You will remember my conversation with him in Rome in 1936 and subsequently I had been present at the Venerable English College when he was consecrated as Archbishop prior to his taking up his appointment in London. It was a great joy to me, therefore, when he attended my first Mass in the Slipper Chapel. As I shall explain, there was a special reason for wanting to say my first Mass in that place. In Rome I had met someone who became a very close friend of mine, Monsignor Bruno Scott James - a great eccentric who outraged some people: I could write books about him. But, he was a very good friend to me because he said "If you are ever at a loose end, I live in a little cottage more or less attached to the Slipper Chapel at Walsingham and although there is no bathroom there and no hot water, there is a good pump in the garden and in the garden I have got three sheds, three wooden summer houses that have been given to me so that I can put up anybody who wants to try out a hermit vocation." I wasn't very keen on being a hermit but I went and stayed every summer for practically the whole of the vacation in the garden of the Slipper Chapel in Walsingham, from 1937 onwards.

So Walsingham, long before my ordination, had become somewhere very special for me and I can tell you all sorts of stories about that. It wasn't an easy life and I had very little money, but Mgr Scott-James was very kind and I used to go in to meals with him. These were somewhat unusual. We would have rusks and honey for breakfast and then by lunchtime when one felt rather hungry, his housekeeper would sometimes bring in just a dish of cornflakes. After a week he himself would get rather hungry and he would say "Get in the car, I'm going to drive you to Lavenham to 'The Swan' and we will have a really good dinner." So off we went to Lavenham and we had an enormous dinner. Well I would have much preferred this to have been spread out over the rest of the week. In between times I used to buy penny bars of chocolate in order to keep going. But, you see apart from all his eccentricity, his madness and his great sense of humour and playing practical jokes, he was a very deeply spiritual man and he taught me more about prayer than anybody I have ever known.

Eventually his regime seemed to have a detrimental effect on his health, perhaps due to undernourishment. As a result some very rich friends of his, first of all bought Stiffkey Hall about 12 miles from Walsingham and asked him to retire there at their expense. So after staying with him in more or less poverty in Walsingham, I used to go and stay with him in baronial splendour. There was a beautiful library and wild duck shoot and a farm. It was like a fairy story really. There he did a lot of writing, notably his translation of the Letters of Saint Bernard; he wrote spiritual books as well and gave a lot of spiritual discourses. Eventually he got rather lonely there and his friends sold Stiffkey Hall and bought for him a house in the village of Downside, near to the Monastery so that he would have the company of the monks and I used to go and stay with him there. That was very pleasant also. So in return when I became, first of all chaplain in London University and then the Administrator of Westminster Cathedral, and had a house at my disposal I could entertain him. It was in Westminster Cathedral clergy house that he found the book by Morris West, *The Children of the Sun,* which told of the work of Don Mario Borelli in the Bassi of Naples. To my amazement, after reading this book, he walked in my room a fortnight later followed by Morris West and Don Mario Borelli, sold up the house at Downside, and went out to help Borelli. He stayed in Italy for many years thereafter. First of all he worked with Borelli and later at the request of the Cardinal Archbishop of Naples he started a hostel for students at the University of Naples who at that time were coming under the influence of the Italian Communists. However he became a very sick man. The College in Naples was closed and he went to live in Rome with the Rosminian Fathers. Cardinal Wright had secured his appointment as a Canon of one of the Roman basilicas, Santa Maria in Trastevere. When he eventually retired he was looked after by the Pensabene family in Rome and in Sussex. He died with them ultimately and is buried at Downside Abbey. I feel a great gratitude to Monsignor Scott James for what he did for me when I was in poverty, so to speak. He used to come every year to stay at Eltofts when I was Bishop of Leeds and he was always a highly entertaining character.

Earlier you spoke of your wish to become a Benedictine when you were received into the Church in 1936. Why did nothing ever come of this desire?

All I can say is that the desire in one sense has persisted all my life. So much so, that even when I retired at the end of 1985 I wondered if it would not still be possible. But at the age of 75 it was clear that it was scarcely practical. In 1985 I did seek Benedictine guidance before accepting the gracious invitation of the Little Sisters of the Poor to retire at the College of the Blessed Virgin in Headingley. I suppose the answer to your question is to be found in the well-known saying of Thomas a Kempis: "Man proposes but God disposes." The pattern of our lives is for Him to decree and not ourselves. In His Providence He called me in all my priestly and episcopal life to other parts of His Vineyard. I think it often happens that the secular clergy are given a love for the great contemplative orders that are an inspiration to them all their lives. This certainly meant much to me regarding the Benedictines and also in my contacts with the Carthusians and Carmelites. And I still look forward eagerly to my annual stay at Downside and sometimes in other Religious houses too.

Why, originally, did you want to enter the Benedictine Order rather than any other?

I think the Benedictine Order is especially attractive to the people of our country because for countless centuries and on account of its innumerable foundations, it became a vital element in the development of what became our Christian civilisation.

There were only two Religious houses in which I had stayed by 1936. They were both Benedictine: Buckfast and Downside. I had therefore not experienced any other form of Religious life. In both places I had received so warm a welcome, and found such peace, that I would have been quite ready to remain in either for the rest of my life. In those days of my Reception it was very rare for a new convert to be allowed to begin postulancy or noviceship in any Religious Order without having first experienced a period as an ordinary Catholic layman in the life of the Church. There was doubtless wisdom in this. However, as you already know, I was surprisingly allowed to go directly to the Beda by Cardinal Hinsley although I had made it clear to him that I really wanted to be a Benedictine. He graciously left me free to tell him or his successor if ever it became clear to me that I wanted to try my vocation in a monastery, and if they thought the time had come to accept me. This never came to be for the reasons I have given you.

Where was your first parish as a Westminster priest?

Following my ordination I was appointed to St Edmund's Church in Lower Edmonton, in July 1940. They were lovely people in that parish and I became extremely devoted to them during my four years with them. It was very much a working-class parish. Obviously the sort of apostolate one did there was YCW. I was very interested in YCW. I had a whole gang of young people involved in this work. I had a very dedicated crowd, lovely people. I am still in touch with some of them after all these years.

My first Parish Priest was Father John George McGrath, who was a very spiritual man. He was also a great disciplinarian and famous for training young curates and life was very strict in the presbytery! For example, as it was wartime there was no hospitality for anyone else because of rationing. When I had friends of mine to see me I had to smuggle them up the back stairs and persuade the housekeeper to make them some spam sandwiches or something like that. But, apart from those sort of things he was a great spiritual example in so many ways. He was very, very strict if one was in one moment after eleven o'clock. One would be reported to the Archbishop for any offence. Of course, in those war days one didn't have much chance to gallivant and I lived there through all the worst days of the London bombings.

I was up many, many nights fire watching apart from anything else and being called to different areas. It was a very difficult time, yet a very happy time. I used to do fire watching with a postman and several young lads. We had sleeping bags on the floor of the school. The postman used to be very generous with endless packets of Wild Woodbine cigarettes. I suppose it was a help enduring all the tensions of the war, but I was rather sorry that I had fallen into the habit again.

By this stage, of course, several years had elapsed since your break with the Anglican Church. You have said that your Father became reconciled to your decision; did he ever visit you in your new home?

At one point while I was at Edmonton my father came and stayed in the presbytery for a day or two because I was quite seriously ill and indeed bulletins were put on the door for people to read saying "Father Wheeler's life is drawing peacefully to a close." This is quite true! Under the sign it said "Please do not knock, please do not ring. His bedroom is just over the front door." Anyway, my father came and a great friendship struck up between him and the very strict parish priest. Looking back I must say I sympathise with Father McGrath because he must have found me rather trying and inexperienced in many ways of Catholic life and in particular he used to be very angry with me for leaving lights on unnecessarily. When another assistant was appointed to St Edmund's he said to the new man "You have been leaving the lights on. I like to analyse what it is that makes you do it. Now with Father Wheeler I know what it is. He was at Oxford and he saw a lot of high life." I think he really thought that the whole of anybody's residence in Oxford was a sort of permanent cabaret! Anyway, he and my father got on extremely well together and after I had recovered and long after my father had gone home he said to me one day "Fine chap your father, pity you took after your mother."

How did you come to leave Edmonton in 1944?

I was rather taken aback when I was asked by Cardinal Griffin to go to Westminster Cathedral to edit the *Westminster Cathedral Chronicle*. The reason he did so was because the previous editor had asked me to write articles on various things for him and when Monsignor Collingwood was made secretary to the Cardinal and was asked to recommend somebody to be editor he suggested me. And so I did as I was told and went there in 1944. I was quite broken hearted because your first parish is always your great love, I suppose, and I was very sorry. Lots of people used to come up from Edmonton to see me at Westminster Cathedral. So for the next six years I edited the *Westminster Cathedral Chronicle* and was on the staff of the Cathedral. I instructed and received a great many converts into the church at that time.

When I left St Edmunds they gave me a presentation as I had been four years in the parish of St Edmunds. And, of course, the parish priest had to make a speech. I was not the only one who wondered very much what he would say and to my great surprise in making the presentation he said "I owe more to Father Wheeler than I can possibly tell you" and I thought "What on earth is he going to say now?" "Owing to the war" he continued "I hardly get any sleep and I find a great consolation in reading and he supplied me, the whole time he was here, with new novels such as I would never have heard about in any other way."

I have often wondered what literature I gave him? I imagine it was the usual Agatha Christie, Evelyn Waugh's specials, Graham Greene, probably Maurice Baring and Galsworthy - with some P. G. Wodehouse thrown in. I have always been surprised by the number of foreigners who have told me how greatly Agatha Christie and P G Wodehouse, with their impeccable English had helped their progress in our language. I remember that one of the first things which Archbishop Heim did when he was appointed Apostolic Delegate and ultimately Pro-Nuncio here, was to invite Agatha Christie to lunch at the Nunciature to thank her for her services to him in that respect.

> ***In 1944 you moved from one extreme to another almost: from a working-class parish to the Metropolitan Cathedral, a church at the centre of Catholic life in the capital.***

Yes, but in those days the Cathedral had a larger parish than it has now and I had quite a large district to cover myself. Most of the people that one visited lived in the Pimlico area of London, which was very run down and a very poor part of the city. But while there was that side to one's ministry as a priest of

Westminster Cathedral one also encountered people from a wide range of backgrounds who came to the Cathedral for various reasons: for the liturgy, for confession, for spiritual direction or for instruction in the Catholic faith.

Of course, at the same time I was also responsible for the *Westminster Cathedral Chronicle*. It was a very good monthly magazine and had quite wide a circulation. It was popular because it had not only Cathedral news but a lot of national news and comment. Unfortunately it no longer exists; but it was always difficult getting the right sort of person to edit it. I always thought of the job as quite secondary to being a curate in the Cathedral. In addition to ordinary parochial duties one had the singing of the whole of the Divine Office, every day. There were some twenty or twenty-two priests there and we were divided into two teams, responsible on alternate weeks for the liturgy which went on at different hours throughout the day. This tied you down very much and you could only interview people, or instruct people or do school or parish visits in between the Divine Office. It was much harder work than an ordinary parish, but also very pleasant for anyone who liked the liturgy. It suited me because the daily High Mass and the offices of Matins, Lauds, Prime, Terce, Sext, None, Vespers and Compline gave a wonderful framework to the day.

> *In your early days at Westminster Cathedral you edited a volume called 'Homage to Newman' to mark the centenary of John Henry Newman's reception into the Catholic Church. I know that Newman has been an important influence on your life, but I wonder how this began?*

I first encountered Newman when as a boy of prep school age I was taken by a school ma'am to a Manchester art gallery. She was deeply anti-Catholic and somewhat distressed, I think, when she found me returning to the Emmeline Deane portrait of Newman. I do not know what really made me spell-bound but there was something holy about it and I wanted to know more about the man. She did not seem to me to share my veneration and it was not until my teens that I learnt more. Music as well as art comes into the picture. My appreciation of Elgar led me to the text itself of *The Dream of Gerontius* and *The Church's Commendation of a departing soul*.

Newman's tradition in Oxford fascinated me; his rooms in Trinity and Oriel, the sculpted portrait in the gardens of Trinity, and above all the University Church of St Mary the Virgin and of course Littlemore with its memory of Blessed Dominic Barberi. I used to cycle there in the days when it was still to some extent a separate village in a country setting. Later, when I was a student in Rome there were frequent visits to the Chiesa Nuova and the old buildings of Propaganda close by the Spanish Steps. I remember accompanying another student, who subsequently became an Oratorian, into the sacristy of San Georgio in Velabro, Newman's titular church, in order to see his portrait. He said, "Non E buono". Of course he meant the picture but the people there naturally thought he was referring to the Cardinal himself and we were hastily shown the door. "Era multo santo", they cried. It made me realise that they had already canonised him in their hearts.

When I was a young priest at Westminster Cathedral I was asked to produce and edit a booklet to mark the centenary of Newman's Reception into the Church for the celebrations on October 9th, 1945. This brought about many Newman friendships for it contained essays by Fr Henry Tristram, Fr Vincent Baker and Fr Vincent Reade of the Oratory as well as Denis Gwynn, Lewis May and others. It also prompted me to make a Newman Pilgrimage in London, Ham near Richmond, Oxford again of course, and Littlemore too; Oscott, Maryvale, Birmingham and Rednall also.

When I became a University Chaplain in 1950 I discovered for the first time the practical riches to be found in *The Idea of a University*. The third and fourth Discourse became especially for me a blue-print regarding the important and essential bearing of Theology on other forms of knowledge. At more or less the same time the realisation of the fundamental significance of the *Grammar of Assent* as a solid foundation of growth became clear in many different contexts. Indeed one became aware of so great a totality of knowledge in Newman so finely and evenly balanced that he was a constant inspiration.

There is a continuity in Newman's philosophical and theological importance throughout his life. In his Anglican period he emphasised the importance of revealed religion (as he also did subsequently in *The Idea of a University*) and of coming to the fullness of the Catholic Faith. In his Catholic period he was utterly loyal to the Church but, at the same time, always defended the just liberties of true scholarship, both clerical and lay, theological and secular against the over-strict line taken by some Ultramontanes. In our own day he is still recalling everyone inside the Church and outside to return to the fullness of Faith and obedience to the duly constituted authority. But at the same time, he is still defending the just liberties of the People of God against anyone who is intransigent.

The spirituality of Newman is an entirely Christocentric one, flowing from his life-long preoccupation with Scripture and the great patristic commentaries. Here again we see his special affinity with Vatican II. This involvement, indeed loving, preoccupation with the Person of Christ, has simplicity as its hallmark. One can understand his undying love for the Grecian simplicity of Trinity College Chapel at Oxford.

Shortly after the end of the Second Vatican Council, I had the joy of being the first Catholic bishop to ascend Newman's pulpit in St Mary the Virgin and to preach the University sermon. From all I have said you will realise how great his influence has been on one individual. And others could tell you far more of his meaning to them.

Did any of your colleagues at Westminster Cathedral in the 1940s become close friends of yours thereafter?

Yes and I think of two men in particular. Monsignor Francis Bartlett is a very great friend of mine and when I became Administrator in 1954 I got him appointed as my sub-Administrator. He was an extraordinary character (from a great London Catholic family) who had been trained for the priesthood in Paris and is therefore bilingual. He is also an authority on Newman, and he has the biggest library of any Catholic priest that I know. He also developed a very deep knowledge of the whole history of the Cathedral and all its art and architecture. He was a mine of information and was a great strength to me. Another priest was 'Father Tommy', Father Thomas Kilcoyne. He was of Irish - Liverpool origin and a lovely character. He became a very close friend of mine right up until the time of his death in 1972. We spent all our holidays together for about a quarter of a century.

Later he was appointed Headmaster of the Choir School in Westminster before he became parish priest first in Gunnersbury and then in Edmonton strangely enough, where he died.

Another character who became, until his death, a very close friend was the late Archbishop David Mathew. Cardinal Hinsley had asked Rome to appoint him as Auxiliary Bishop in the later thirties. Born of a devoted Catholic family he tried his vocation, as a Carthusian at Parkminster after graduation from Oxford as a historian of standing and a period in the Navy, but ultimately he became a secular priest and was actually one of my predecessors in the London University assignment. When I was a priest in the forties at Westminster, he lived close by the Cathedral in Carlisle Place and was exceptionally kind to people like myself. Billy Clonmore was a great friend of his and George Temple also. In fact he introduced me to a great many of his friends, beginning with his devoted Dominican brother Father Gervase Mathew OP who was a lecturer in Byzantine studies at Oxford. They were inseparable and many delightful stories, some *ben trovato*, were told about them. David encouraged me with my writing and was responsible for my becoming a Chaplain of the Knights of Malta and also being elected to The Athenaeum. Cardinal Griffin did not ask for him to continue as Auxiliary. In fact, he wanted the Holy See to appoint Canon George Craven in his place and Rome moved David to be Apostolic Delegate in East Africa with the title of Archbishop and a residence at Mombasa. This made the continuation of his historical researches in the British Museum and elsewhere no longer possible and turned his genius to a trilogy of novels on the post war period dealing with the salaried classes, the leisured classes in *The Mango on the Mango Tree* and *In Vallambrosa* and the proletariat in *The Prince of Wales Feathers*. These gave great delight to his friends. But he will be remembered especially for his historical works especially those relating to the Navy and the Stuarts. Ultimately, on return from Africa in which he had great impact, he became for a time Bishop to the Forces before retiring as Chaplain to the Camoys family at Stonor. He played a considerable part in Pope John XXIII's preparations for the Council but as far as I can remember did not attend the Sessions. It was a great privilege to know him and he ever remained the loyalest of friends. I was glad to be asked to pay tribute to him at his Requiem in Westminster Cathedral.

There are, of course, others in my Westminster days about whom I could reminisce with affection: Douglas and Mia Woodruff who kept ever open house in Carlisle Place before they moved to Marcham Priory where I joined them on many happy occasions including Douglas' 80th birthday celebrations. Many of my contemporaries will remember Michael Ramsey's first visit to Westminster Cathedral as ecumenism opened new doors and a memorable friendship with him and his wife, Joan. Our Cathedral Art Commission included such figures as Sir John Rothenstein, Arthur Pollen, Professor Bodkin, and Goodhart Rendel. They were all regular visitors to the Clergy House as indeed were Arthur Fleischmann and his wife Joy who often visited me later in Middlesbrough and Leeds. For many years I was on the executive of the Converts Aid Society which promoted a long and devoted relationship with Freddy and Pat Chambers. The late Sir Lennox and Lady Lennox-Berkeley and their family have always remained close friends. And then there were the Auxiliary Bishops of Westminster: Bishop George Craven of St James, Spanish Place, Archbishop Myers of St Mary's Cadogan Street and later Bishop David Cashman, Patrick Casey and Victor Guazzelli. The last named had been on my staff at Westminster. And amongst the Westminster priests, Mgr Reginald Butcher and Mgr Vernon Johnson were both close friends. Canon Adrian Arrowsmith, now at Our Lady of Victories, Kensington, who was also on the Cathedral staff in my time, has kept up a close and devoted friendship. There must be many others who through the years have kept up a regular contact. All the world seemed to come to Westminster Cathedral because it was so central. And I always felt there that the Good Lord had used me as a signpost - a role that so many of us on that staff fulfilled: ships that pass in the night, if you like. And beyond all count are they. May they forgive my omissions and sometimes my forgetfulness.

I must tell you of an incident which happened during this period when I was a young priest. I was called out of the confessional on a Saturday night by somebody telling me that the organist for Benediction was ill and they knew that I could play the *O Salutaris* and *Tantum Ergo* and would I please play it for the Benediction at 8 o'clock. So this I did and it went on for some weeks because the illness of the regular organist was prolonged. Each week I got somewhat bolder not only playing the *O Salutaris* and the *Tantum Ergo* but also a little voluntary by way of introduction as they came out and so forth. One night however I was told afterwards that there were two priests waiting to go in for Benediction when the clock struck eight and one said to the other as they heard me playing a rather lively voluntary "What does this remind you of?" and the other one replied "I really don't know." And the first one said "Would you say a seaside landlady entertaining her lodgers on a wet Sunday afternoon?" I tried to get out of this assignment after that!

In 1950 you were appointed by Cardinal Griffin to be the Roman Catholic chaplain to the University of London. Why were you chosen for this work?

Because I was one of the few secular priests who had been to an English university in those days. There were lots of people who had been to continental universities, but not to English ones. It meant of course that I had to step down from the editorship of the *Cathedral Chronicle* because that had to be done from Westminster.

At first there wasn't any accommodation either for the chaplaincy or the Chaplain! Cardinal Griffin said he wanted me to buy a centre for the University Chaplaincy because my predecessor had lived in the basement of the Newman Society House in Portman Square (now the site of the Churchill Hotel). So, the first thing I had to do was to look around for a property and I bought, with Diocesan money, a beautiful Adams house in Devonshire Place near Regent's Park. It was difficult to decide where the centre should be because London colleges were so scattered. It was certainly not an appointment I would ever have chosen myself. It wasn't like Oxford or Cambridge where all the colleges were together. They could be as far as 25 miles apart. It seemed that it was necessary to do two things: to have a central grouping and a diasporate grouping which meant having individual Catholic Societies in individual colleges. As a result I was travelling around all over the place.

The property in Devonshire Place was a dream of a house and became a great focal centre for all the colleges in Central London. I used to borrow from the Rosminian Fathers, the Church of St Etheldreda's, Ely Place on a Sunday and Holydays of Obligation, for an Academic Mass. Mgr Ronald Knox preached at the first of these events. We also continued the annual Academic Mass each autumn in Westminster Cathedral which was always a very unifying event. There were lots of other happenings as well during term, and a great many students were married there during my time as Chaplain. The Chaplaincy became a great social centre. We had a small chapel in which we had daily Masses and small group Masses.

Considerable numbers gathered there mostly from the colleges in the central London Area and some excellent programmes were laid on both by the students and the graduates. Professor George Temple was a great source of strength to me. Later on he held a Chair in Oxford and after the death of his wife became a monk at Quarr Abbey in the Isle of Wight. It was a great joy in later years to greet him as a monk and a priest.

The Chaplaincy was also supported by different groups financially. In the early days there were problems though Cardinal Griffin was a tower of strength and especially in asking the Viscount Furness, who had just become of age, to help support the London Chaplaincy. I owe a great debt of gratitude to Tony Furness for his loyal and devoted kindness to me in the Chaplaincy and ever afterwards. Amongst other things we devised a way by which the upper rooms of the Chaplaincy could be 'let out' to lodgers who could afford to pay a rent which could assist the maintenance of the place. Obviously, the ideal was to have priests who could enter to some extent into the Catholic life of the place. And so we had in residence some of the Vicars General of the Forces who had high government salaries.

As a priest I missed ordinary parish life to some extent and usually went to supply in the long vacation each year at Our Lady of Ransom, Eastbourne. On one occasion, however, the Vicar General of the Army Mgr Clarke, who lived with us in the Chaplaincy, asked me if I would make a tour of the British Army on the Rhine, giving retreats to chaplains and officers and men in different areas. This was a fascinating tour beginning at Herdecke near Dortmund, leading on to Monchengladbach and Cologne. Thence to Bielefeld and Bad Oeynhausen, ending up in Berlin - and, in those days before the wall, - walking through the Brandenburg Gate for a short tour of the already existing eastern zone. All the transport was laid on by the army, mostly by way of long train journeys and usually accompanied by a senior officer. It was a rewarding experience.

It was also during this period that I paid my first visit to the U.S.A. This took place a little before I became Administrator of the Cathedral at Westminster. I had been invited to give a lecture on Newman in New York. And I took the opportunity subsequently of visiting Graymoor which I knew to be the Mother House of the Franciscans of the Atonement near to Garrison in the Catskill area of New York State. I had been invited by Father Angelus Delahunt who was at that time the General of the Order which had begun its life in the Episcopal Church and in the early years of the century had been received corporately into the Catholic Church rather like the monks of Caldey Island. The Founder was Father Paul Wattson who had started *The Chair of Unity Octave* (January 18th - 25th) which was a prayer crusade and in the time of Pope Benedict XV it was extended to the Universal Church.

Father Angelus offered later to make a Westminster Foundation to save the sinking Catholic Central Library. He was a person of amazing generosity and became a very devoted friend. On subsequent occasions I was invited, all expenses paid, to visit the U.S.A. and was escorted not only to Graymoor and New York but also to Washington DC, Virginia, Chicago and many other places. It was a wonderful experience of the hospitality and generosity of the American people and I made many new friends. Father Angelus stayed with us sometimes in London and was taken to Oxford and Cambridge, Canterbury, Arundel and other places. He took great pride in the London foundation and his successors have always been faithful to the lead which he gave.

In 1953 you were made Ecclesiastical Adviser to the Union of Catholic Students. This appointment was to outlive your stay at the London University Chaplaincy.

Indeed it was, because even when I was Administrator at Westminster Cathedral I still carried on in this post until 1960. The chief thing that it involved was the summer school as I had to go every year to the summer school in different parts of the country, organised by the Union of Catholic Students. They were lovely gets-together with the students, although I was never one for wanting to stay up all night like so many students are! It was also interesting to meet Bishops of different dioceses and other chaplains. We started the idea of a Conference of University Chaplains when I was chaplain to London University. The first meeting of all was held in Devonshire Place in our chaplaincy. The most outstanding chaplain of those days was Mgr Gilbey from Cambridge, and we elected him as the first Chairman of the university chaplains' conference.

In 1954 you returned to Westminster Cathedral as Administrator. How did this appointment come about?

On January 25th I was rung up by Cardinal Griffin who told me that the previous Administrator, Monsignor Collingwood, had decided to retire following an outcry in *The Times* newspaper regarding the removal of a pillar from the Cathedral which was considered by the world of art and architecture as entirely unnecessary and in fact a distortion of the original Bentley plan. The Cardinal had been very upset about it and determined to set up a council of selected authorities to advise those responsible for the edifice in subsequent years. This was a wise suggestion and it has been implemented now for many years.

This was the scene of my inauguration as Administrator. I suppose the Cardinal realised that I had already known the life of the Cathedral for six years previous to the London University Chaplaincy. He knew too that I had a great love for the liturgy and everything connected therewith. In the first instance it was not an easy assignment on account of the circumstances and there was some misunderstanding about my predecessor's retirement. But I was greatly supported from the very start in all that I did. And so began a challenging but rewarding ten years.

How would you describe the role of Administrator?

One has the tremendous responsibility of looking after the Cathedral itself, and then one has to supervise a very large staff; Westminster had twenty-two priest assistants in my time. So, one had to manage people and all the other resources which are needed in the life of the Cathedral. But, in another sense I would liken my role there in the late 1950's and early sixties to that of

Abbot in a small monastery. You see all my work was greatly enriched by the daily round of liturgy and I tried to participate in it much more than had been done before.

> *You served three Archbishops. Cardinal Griffin for two years or thereabouts, Cardinal Godfrey for seven years from 1956 to 1963 and then briefly from 1963 to 1964, Cardinal Heenan. Did they give you a free hand to operate as Administrator?*

Yes, all of them. I always kept very closely in touch with them and when I was going to make any radical change I always consulted them before doing so. In all this Monsignor Derek Worlock, now Archbishop of Liverpool, was a very great help to me in his capacity as Archbishop's Secretary. If they said no, I accepted it. Cardinal Griffin backed me up through thick and thin, both at the London Chaplaincy and the Cathedral and I was always very grateful for that. Cardinal Godfrey was always very kind, but it was a very different regime. It was known as the "safe period". Cardinal Heenan likewise was always very kind to me but I knew he thought that the whole of Westminster wanted a very new look. He asked me who should succeed me when I went to be coadjutor Bishop of Middlesbrough. I said "I would appoint my sub-Administrator, Francis Bartlett". "No," he said, "I am not going to appoint him, he is to be appointed to the Church of the Assumption in Warwick Street. Is there anyone else that you would suggest?" I said "Well, Mgr Tomlinson has succeeded me at the London University Chaplaincy. He has been there now for 10 years. I suppose he is of the right calibre". And so he appointed him, but after a few years moved him to St James, Spanish Place and Francis Bartlett was appointed as Administrator in 1967.

> *One of your priorities as Administrator was to make Westminster Cathedral a more effective pastoral centre. How did you go about your task after 1954?*

Before I explain what I did, perhaps I should say something about the history of the Cathedral itself so that what happened can be placed in context.

Cardinal Vaughan, the third Archbishop of Westminster, was the one who founded Westminster Cathedral. He not only founded the building, he founded the whole liturgical round and a constitution was drawn up by him whereby the priests of the Cathedral spent a great deal of their day performing the liturgy in much the same way that monks do in monasteries. In fact, Cardinal Vaughan had tried very hard to get Benedictines to begin the liturgical life of Westminster Cathedral, but that never came off. He decided, therefore, that he was going to form groups of secular priests who would perform the whole liturgical round of the Church's worship daily. That consisted of all the different liturgical hours of the day: Matins, Lauds, Prime, Terce, Sext, None, Vespers and Compline. This was divided into three big sessions in the Cathedral itself and the centre of them all was the daily High Mass which took place every morning at 10.30 and was preceded by the office of Prime and Terce.

So Cardinal Vaughan established the great liturgical round at the Cathedral which made it from the first a great power-house in the Metropolis. Of course, this led over the years to a good deal of stricture regarding the clergy of Westminster Cathedral. For example, a lot of other priests said they were wasting their time reciting all these prayers and not getting on with the pastoral duties of the place and some laity I suppose would have thought the same. But, in these days when the whole life of prayer, especially priestly prayer, is considered as a *sine qua non* of Christian life, it is perhaps appreciated in a different way. Nevertheless the great liturgical round of Westminster Cathedral has gone on: though in a somewhat different way dictated by the requirements of new circumstances.

I was anxious, when I became Administrator, to maintain the great liturgical tradition and to be present myself as often as all my other obligations allowed. There were many other obligations because the Cathedral always had a parish, and there were also a number of hospitals. It was a centre for all sorts of organisations and became a natural centre for anyone wanting to find out anything about the Catholic Church. Therefore, there seemed to me to be a great opportunity for a fuller combination of the liturgical and the pastoral sides of the Cathedral's life. One of the things that I did was to ensure the presence of the clergy in the confessionals, throughout the day, at least one all day and at busy times several. This needed a considerable amount of commitment on the part of the clergy and of organisation on the part of the Administrator. But it brought new life to the Cathedral because there were always queues of people waiting for confession and we did everything we could to help this situation which seemed to be an entirely pastoral development. I am not saying that this hadn't gone on before in a desultory sort of way but now it became an essential part of the whole place. Therefore there was a new life which developed in the Cathedral with the wonderful cooperation of the twenty-two assistants which the Administrator had at that time.

I emphasise "at that time" because it has not been easy in latter years for many obvious reasons to maintain that great number of priests. Nevertheless, the tradition by and large has continued. I would want to say that I don't claim any kudos for that. Everybody felt the same, we had long discussions about it and decided by dialogue how it could best be implemented and so from the start there was a very close and very happy relationship between myself and the staff there. I found it a great advantage that I had had experience at the Cathedral previously myself, knew where everything was, and was aware of a lot of the things that needed to be done and that now could be done. This involved a great deal of delegation and trust. It meant delegating and delegating, giving those delegated their head: but never abdicating.

Westminster Cathedral, of course, is a very distinctive building; was it a church which appealed to you aesthetically?

Oh yes, I have always loved Westminster Cathedral. From the first time I ever went into it as a non-Catholic, I was swept off my feet. It has an extraordinary ethos of spiritual power and the mystery of the God-head, in fact a tremendous atmosphere of prayer. The Cathedral always "takes over" and anything banal is somehow spiritually excluded. Externally it has been tremendously enhanced by Westminster Council's great achievement of the Piazza at the west front. Older people will remember how the Cathedral was hidden away at the back of Victoria Street. Now it is one of the splendid monuments of London and is illuminated at night and creates an unforgettable impression. It also provided a marvellous arrival point for the Holy Father when he came to England in 1982.

In what ways did you try to enhance the interior of the Cathedral during your time as Administrator?

My first priority on being appointed was to take the opportunity at a time when costs were not too high, of doing something towards completing the interior of the building. One has to remember that Cardinal Vaughan decided to build Westminster Cathedral in a style that didn't attempt to compete in any way with the Gothic of Westminster Abbey or the Classical of St Paul's Cathedral. That is why he choose Bentley to erect a Byzantine edifice on the lines of Santa Sophia in Constantinople. His design for the interior warranted completion in revetment marble to a certain height topped by a vast range of mosaics in the individual chapels and in all the great domes.

As the Cardinal had requested, I appointed a group of well known architects and artists to advise on what ought to be done to the interior of the Cathedral. They were all convinced that there should be the completion of the design as Cardinal Vaughan and Bentley had intended and so one of the first things to do was to plan the marbling revetment. I was very fortunate here in having the assistance of my sub-Administrator, subsequently Monsignor Provost Bartlett, because he had a knowledge of marble and on several occasions travelled to Greece to make sure that several important kinds of marble were still available. We started with one bay, at the West End of the Cathedral, as it was going to cost a considerable amount of money. We launched a fund called the 'Million Crown Fund' which was organised by one of the priests, with the help of a lay secretary. This first instalment was quickly paid for and we were able to go onto the next. I am amazed still that this process continued until all the different arches along the whole length of the Cathedral had been completed in the way that the architect originally intended. There was then the question of a great balustrade. This arose because there was a triforium which had only a wooden railing running along the edge. This always seemed very unsafe when people crowded up there on the big occasions. Apart from that, it was part of the original design that this should all be marble. As a result the balustrade on both sides of the Nave was completed.

When we came to the question of mosaics we got in touch with one of the most famous workers in mosaic, at that time, Boris Anrep, and through our Art Commission he was engaged to do the mosaics in the Blessed Sacrament Chapel. This cost, even in those days, a considerable sum of money and made it absolutely clear that it was going to be impossible ever in our time to do anything about mosaicing the great domes. There were many different theories about this on the part of the art commission, but there was a general feeling that probably the problem would only ultimately be solved when somebody had been clever enough to invent the right kind of mosaic spray. As far as I know this has never effectively happened. Little, therefore, has been done about the mosaics. However the Chapel of St Paul has been completed and there have been a few panels inset in the marble frames which had been created as a result of the marble revetment.

There are other things that are very notable, such as the Shrine of the young St Therese de Lisieux to whom Cardinal Griffin was specially devoted. We got Giacomo Manzu, who had done the bronze doors of the Vatican, to design a bronze plaque of St Therese which is now in the Lady Chapel of Westminster Cathedral.

Mention must also be made of Roy de Maistre's Stations of the Cross in the long corridor linking the Clergy House, Archbishop's House, and the Choir School with the Sacristy of the Cathedral. The artist was a well-known convert of the late Father Alfonso de Zulueta and he invited me often to his studio in Eccleston Street. All his works are now becoming much better known and are highly prized. When the Stations were completed, a reception was held especially for the Art World in the Great Corridor.

One of the other great ornaments to be added (and thereby hangs many an interesting tale) was the setting up of the beautiful alabaster shrine of Our Lady of Westminster underneath Gill's thirteenth Station of the Cross. This alabaster had become the *piece de resistance* in an Antique Dealers fair after it had been bought from a French family by the ecclesiastical art dealer, Wolsey. It was an English alabaster of Our Lady and the Holy Child dating from the 15th century and when we heard about it we were all very interested because there had always been different theories about pre-Reformation statues being secretly shipped abroad.

It was a very beautiful piece and Cardinal Griffin was so anxious to have it that he gave me a cheque to go along to Wolsey and to buy it. When I got there Wolsey told me that, alas, he couldn't let me have it because the Dean of York had bespoken it for York Minster and had started a fund to buy it. So far, however, he had only got one donation of £1,000 from Sir William Milner, who was a great benefactor of York Minster. So I said "Well of course I understand the situation. But if the arrangement were to fall through, I would be very grateful if you would let me know." Some months passed and one day I went into Wolsey's place again and said "I see the statue is still there, and has not gone to York." He said "Oh, I was about to let you know that I have had a letter from the Dean of York saying that he has got no further donations apart from the one from Sir William Milner, and if Westminster Cathedral still want it, he thinks that Westminster Cathedral should have it. I am therefore now in a position to let you buy it." Accordingly this took place and the alabaster was inaugurated and blessed by Archbishop Edward Myers, as Cardinal Griffin was ill at the time. The Dean of York was represented, appropriately, by Sir William Milner at the installation of the Shrine on the Feast of the Immaculate Conception in 1955. Since then it has become a great centre of devotion. Iconographists have linked it with the pre-Reformation statue in Westminster Abbey of Our Lady of the Pew. One person gave us a silver altar to place in front of it. I gather that subsequent generations have thought that it would be better to have an open space in front of it with room for votive candles and flowers. And the silver altar now has a place of honour in the Crypt of the Cathedral.

There was also a great development musically, especially during the long and outstanding regime of George Malcolm, as the Master of Music. He built up the notable post-war tradition of the choir, liturgically, and traditionally in the line of the chant but also in that of polyphony and the classics together with the best of modern developments. For example, I can remember Britten coming to the Cathedral to compose his Mass for the choir and bursting into tears when he heard the boys singing it for the first time, not because he was disappointed but because he was overcome with the beauty that they infused into his work. The Malcolm tradition was carried on magnificently by others and especially Colin Mawby.

Westminster Cathedral is the focal point for Catholic life in the capital and indeed nationally. This must have resulted in many varied and interesting experiences for you during your time as Administrator. One of these, I believe, concerns a visit to London by President Kennedy.

Yes, I was rung up one day by the Princess Radziwill who asked me if I could arrange for the baptism of her infant son to take place in the drawing room at their house in Buckingham Gate. I replied that I wondered why they wanted it in their own house, and why not in the Cathedral? "Well" she said "as a matter of fact, my brother-in-law, the President of the United States, is coming over on a private visit in order to be godfather to my son and of course the question of security will arise." So I said to her "I shall have to discuss this with Cardinal Godfrey, but I think it is extremely unlikely that permission will be granted because this is always rather a special occasion and the Cardinal will want to know very clearly why it isn't taking place in a Catholic church." She then pointed out that royal baptisms of the House of Windsor were held in the drawing room of Buckingham Palace. When I mentioned this to Cardinal Godfrey he did not take the parallel very seriously but thought it would be better if we could persuade them to have the baptism, perhaps if not in the Cathedral itself, then in the Crypt.

This was eventually the decision made and I can remember shortly afterwards, and long before the event, a whole bevy of American security men coming into my room and asking me to give them full details of the lay-out of the Cathedral so that there could be absolute security for the event. It was decided that the President should enter via the Clergy House at the back of the Cathedral, in Francis Street, and, of course, I met him and his wife at the door with their suite and took them through the great corridor from the Clergy House into the Cathedral and down the steps to the Crypt Chapel. Just before this happened I had been down into the Crypt to see if everything was arranged as I had requested. I had been told by the security men that they were particularly frightened of photographers and they didn't want any photographers in the place at all, an instruction I passed on to the Cathedral sacristans. You can imagine my surprise, therefore, to find a photographer about to plug his lighting into an electric point. I advanced towards him, whereupon one of the sacristans came up to me and said "This one is all right, Monsignor." I said "What do you mean it is all right. I have given strict orders about this." "Ah yes" he said "but this is Mrs Kennedy's private photographer who escorts her out shopping and is allowed everywhere." So having checked upon this I found that it was permissible. I remember now how very friendly and informal and pleasant both the Kennedys and all their suite were. As we went down in to the Crypt the President genuflected before the Blessed Sacrament, despite the difficulty in so doing caused I think by some spinal affliction. But he did so and played his part, just as any other godparent, as I performed the baptism. Once this was over we proceeded to the common room, in the clergy house with the newly baptised baby in the arms of a member of the family. There the Cardinal was waiting to meet everyone and the Kennedys asked him to consecrate the child to Our Lady. And so the statue of Our Lady was brought in from my own study and the consecration was made. Afterwards we were all invited to a reception at the Radziwills house in Buckingham Gate and it was a very interesting gathering as you can imagine. I can remember the Prime Minister, Harold MacMillan, being there, for example, and many other distinguished people. Afterwards the Radziwills together with the Kennedys went to Buckingham Palace for dinner. It was not very long afterwards that the tragic assassination of President Kennedy occurred and we were all very sad about this and even the boys in the Choir School who had been rewarded with a whole day's holiday by him for singing at the baptism, showed their sympathy to the American Ambassador when he came for the Requiem in the Cathedral.

Such events can be memorable for quite different reasons. One embarrassing incident happened during that time when so many different countries in the world were becoming independent with the end of colonialism. Most of the Catholic countries wanted to come to Westminster Cathedral for a Solemn High Mass with their Ambassadors present and ministers from their governments to celebrate their new freedom. We had a number of these occasions and I remember one attended by a large congregation from a Spanish speaking country. It had been arranged, therefore, that a Spanish priest should come and preach the sermon in their own language. We had a Solemn Latin High Mass and I was in the stalls of the Cathedral. Next to me was Bishop Cashman who was an auxiliary Bishop of Westminster representing the Cardinal for the occasion. When the moment came for the Homily to begin there was no sign of the Spanish priest and a message from the sacristy informed me that he had not arrived. I turned to Bishop Cashman and said "My Lord, they have just told me that the man who is supposed to be giving the Spanish Homily has not come, will you say a few words to these people?" "Oh no" he said "that will be for you to do." The great problem was I could not for the life of me think what country it was or to whom I was speaking. And yet it was essential that something should be done at that juncture. So I went to the microphone and said, addressing the Ambassador and the congregation, "Your Excellency, I know that this is a very great day for your country and we wish it every blessing on the independence that has now been granted to it. This will mean great new dedication from you and all your people" and went on in that sort of way without committing myself to any names. It was very difficult to sustain this for any length of time but apparently it went off all right because in the sacristy afterwards the Ambassador came in and said "Monsignor, we are so delighted that the Spanish preacher didn't arrive because we would never have had that wonderful message from you for our country." I felt deeply embarrassed by this but I hope the good Lord will forgive me because I only tried to do my best to help the situation.

Old age sometimes precipitates forgetfulness and I would like to tell you of a more recent *faux pas*. It happened when the Duchess of Kent was unveiling a plaque commemorating the 30th anniversary of the coming of the Graymoor Friars to London to save the Catholic Central Library from closure. I had been instrumental in persuading Cardinal Godfrey to invite them and looked after them when they came. I had, therefore, to make a little speech of thanks. Now I should tell you that all of us in Yorkshire think of the Duchess in the context of our own county where she is very dear to everybody. But instead of addressing her at the start of my speech as the Duchess of Kent, I did so as the "Duchess of York". This brought the house down and I must say that the Duchess of Kent took it in very good part. She said to me "I think you made that little mistake because last time you saw me was in York." And I said, "No, Your Royal Highness, the last time I saw you was not in York but at Leeds University when as Chancellor you bestowed a degree upon me. I am sure everybody here this evening will now realise that in no way did I deserve it!"

The Bishop of Leeds greeting His Holiness Pope John Paul II on his arrival at the Knavesmire, York, 31st May 1982.

The Bishop with his late father on the lawn of Bishop's House, 'Eltofts', at Thorner.

Many amusing things happened at Westminster. One morning I was at the back of Westminster Cathedral and an elderly and *ancien regime* lady, with a walking stick came in and asked me if I would be so good as to hear her confession. Of course I said "Yes, perhaps you would come into one of these confessional boxes over here." To which she replied "I think that I should tell you that I am usually afforded the courtesy of a chair when I go to confession" (Which in those days was very unusual). So I thought "This is rather difficult because all these chairs in the nave of the Cathedral seem to be battened together, I can scarcely bring a whole row of them over to the confessional. What can I do?" So we walked down the Cathedral together towards the Lady Chapel and I suddenly got an idea. In an ambulacrum by the side of the Lady Chapel is a special confessional for deaf people, far away from all the others and so I took her into this ambulacrum. There was nobody about and so I opened the door of the priest's part of the confessional and told her to go in and sit down and I myself went round to the penitent's side, where I had to kneel and heard her confession. She kept me on my knees for quite a long time but eventually it was over and we both opened the doors and came out. Of course, it would happen that at that moment I was seen by one member of the Cathedral staff who spread it round the diocese that the Administrator was going for spiritual direction to a certain lady who was very *ancien regime*.

> *We have been talking about your various responsibilities as Administrator of Westminster Cathedral. During your years at Westminster were there certain places to which you retreated, literally, from this busy life to enjoy spiritual refreshment?*

Of course, I have returned to Downside almost every year, since I became a Catholic in 1936, to have a retreat there and to say Mass in the Lady Chapel where I was received. But, there was another monastery that was always a great inspiration to me and especially in the days when I was a priest in Westminster. I refer to the great Carthusian Monastery of Parkminster in Sussex, near Horsham. That very large monastery was built by the emigre Carthusians from France at the end of the nineteenth century and was readily accessible from Westminster. I was always interested in the life of that order because it is quite different from the

Cenobitic Orders, in that it is fundamentally a solitary vocation. It is really a continuation of the life of the desert fathers because those who are called to this very unusual vocation, live a solitary life each in a little house off the cloisters. They rarely meet apart from the Chapel and there is almost perpetual silence. Most of the day is spent either in prayer or in manual work, and sometimes in literary work as it was in the case of Archbishop Mathew when he was there. I often tell the story of a priest of the Middlesbrough diocese who went to Parkminster and was already a Carthusian Monk when I had the privilege of knowing him. I have always had the most tremendous regard for the depth of his spirituality. He was a very upstanding character who loved football matches and loved beautiful music and all the good things of life. One year he went on holiday with a couple of priests, who were friends of his, down to Sussex. In the course of their tour they called in at Parkminster and were taken round the great cloister and into one of the houses which was empty. When they came out again my friend seemed to be very silent and somewhat morose. The other two said "Well, that's a rather terrifying place, isn't it? Let's go and have a drink somewhere." So they went to have a drink but it didn't seem to make very much difference to him. They said "What's wrong with you? Something seems to have got to you in that place?" To which he replied "Well, it's all very well for you fellows but I have got to go back there." They said "What, you go back to be a Carthusian? We have never heard anything so ridiculous in our lives. You are not at all the type to be called to a religious life." "Well," he said "I will have to try it at any rate." He did go there and he persevered and became a model Carthusian. He was a wonderful person and he died eventually in the odour of sanctity at a Carthusian monastery in Italy.

When I met him in the late forties he was a full Carthusian monk. I asked him what had happened when he visited Parkminster. He said to me "Well you know these little houses, there are two rooms on the ground floor and a little garden, where you do gardening. There is wood shed where you do manual work. Then there is a corridor leading up to a staircase and the staircase brings you into two rooms on the first floor where the Carthusian monk spends most of his life because not all his prayers are said in the Church. His whole life is prayer and it is the strictest of all the Orders. Indeed it is said that the Carthusian order has never had to be reformed because it never became necessary." He continued: "You probably remember that at the top of the stairs of this little house, in every house, there is a plain wooden cross. As I walked up those stairs I heard a voice saying to me "Will you nail yourself to this cross for me?" It was a naked cross not a crucifix. I said "What did you say in reply?" "I said, oh no Lord, but if it is your will, I must say yes." And so he came. I then said to him "Did you find that having come here and having done your best to nail yourself to that cross that it was something done once and for all and that everything in the garden was beautiful ever after?" "No" he said "I have to nail myself anew every morning." To meet such a person was one of the great inspirations of my life and I believe now that he is praying for me at the throne of God.

By 1961 you had been a Roman Catholic for twenty-five years and a priest for over twenty. Would you say the Church had changed at all during those years?

Fundamentally, and of its nature, the Church remains ever the same. Nevertheless, I never thought that there would be the sort of changes that there subsequently were.

Having an historical mind I found it a difficult period later in the 1960s, especially when the liturgical reforms happened. I thought many of them were unnecessary and yet I never for a moment thought of departing from what the Universal Church had decided. I've always felt perfectly happy as long as I am going hand in hand with the successors of St Peter and the Apostles. For this reason it never worried me at all that he should be calling a Council because after all there had been twenty General Councils of the Church. These had been very much a part of its life, theologically, spiritually and in every way. So I wasn't alarmed at all when John XXIII decided to "open a window" so to speak. Also, one realised from a historical point of view that Vatican I had broken up through the Franco-Prussian War before it had really completed its agenda. There was something to be said for the completion of that agenda, so it never worried me that the Pope should be calling a second Vatican Council.

Looking back on this period, how would you assess Pope John XXIII?

He was a glorious character. I met him on various occasions and one thing that always impressed me about him was that whenever you went into an audience with him, and saw him going round all the different groups of people there was one word that always stood out: "Coraggio, Coraggio, Coraggio!" - "Have courage." It was very refreshing to see him walking into the Second Vatican Council accompanied by his entourage because he looked just like a very nice old farmer taking a look at his crops and seeing how the cattle and sheep were getting on. He really was a most lovable person and there were all sorts of stories about him that illustrated this. When somebody asked him how many people worked in the Vatican he said "About half of them". And the other story I like is about him going for a walk in the afternoon in the Vatican gardens attended by one of his assistants. He saw that a group of gardeners were being moved out of the way. So he said to the Monsignor "Why are all those gardeners being huddled out of this place?" and the Monsignor replied "For security reasons, your Holiness." And he thought for a moment, and then said, "Well I wasn't going to do anything to them." Subsequently I have been on a pilgrimage to his birthplace Sotto il Monte, near Bergamo up in the North of Italy, and it has really become almost a shrine. He certainly was a God-given inspiration to the Church of our time.

The Second Vatican Council began in the Autumn of 1962 and then in the following June, of course, John XXIII died after just one session and was succeeded by Paul VI. Was the election of Cardinal Montini something you had expected?

Yes. We all thought that when Pius XII died the Archbishop of Milan would be made Pope although he wasn't a Cardinal. The Cardinals at that time, no doubt under the guidance of the Holy Spirit, decided they weren't going to have somebody who wasn't already a Cardinal. Pius XII never made Archbishop Montini a Cardinal. After the Conclave, one of the first things that John XXIII did was to remedy that. So I think it is a notable sign of God's intervention in history that things happened the way that they did. I'm quite sure that the election of Pope Paul VI was entirely providential - I have never had any doubts about that.

Early in the following year you were appointed as Coadjutor Bishop of Middlesbrough, thus bringing to an end a ten year period as Administrator of Westminster Cathedral. I believe you were informed of your new appointment on 25th January 1964, exactly ten years to the day since Cardinal Griffin had asked you to become Administrator. Can we assume that by the beginning of 1964 you knew that it was probable that you would become a bishop before too long?

That is not an easy question to answer because one is not free to divulge matters of confidentiality. This particular appointment was however a great surprise when it came. It was on the 25th January 1964 that I was invited to lunch with Archbishop Cardinale at the Apostolic Delegation. When I got there I found that he wanted a session with me alone before lunch and to my great surprise he said "The Holy Father would like you to become the Coadjutor Bishop of Middlesbrough, in Yorkshire. Would you be ready to say Volo or Nolo - Yes or no, to that." Well I was rather taken aback and he said "Do you want to have time to think about it?". I said "No, I wouldn't want any time to think about anything that the Holy Father had asked me to do." He looked very relieved that I wasn't raising any obstacles and so then I asked him to tell me more about it.

Although I had been born in Yorkshire, I had been brought up in Lancashire, and later spent many years at the family home in Sussex. Then I had been for 24 years a priest of the Westminster Diocese. So this appointment was rather out of the blue and to be quite frank, when I got back to my room in Westminster Cathedral I had to take the map out to find out where Middlesbrough was. I knew York and parts of the West Riding but I had never been to Teesside. So it was all quite an extraordinary experience for me. It was complicated by the fact that when one is told that kind of news it is sometimes two or three weeks before you are allowed to say a word to anybody about it. I had to keep silent about the matter from January 25th to February 11th which was almost three weeks. It was announced publicly on the feast of Our Lady of Lourdes, and I remember on that morning I went up to Cardinal Heenan's study and had permission to tell him that my new appointment was going to be announced. He then said "Oh well, after 12 o'clock I will come down to the common room at the Clergy House and tell them what's happening" and he came and put a zucchetto on my head which was apparently the custom.

What was your first introduction to the Middlesbrough Diocese?

After the announcement of my appointment it was arranged that I would go to Middlesbrough and visit Bishop Brunner to whom I was to be coadjutor. He gave me a wonderfully kind reception and I always regarded him as a very gentle person. I went up there and asked him what he wanted me to do. He had a great sense of humour and he said "Oh, I don't know, we'll have to think about that," which seemed rather surprising to me in view of the fact that he had asked for a coadjutor. So eventually I said to him "Where do you want me to reside?" They had told me in the Apostolic Delegation that they thought he was keeping a parish in Hull vacant for me. It was clear that there are two very different parts of the Middlesbrough Diocese - Teesside and Humberside, and it perhaps needed a presence on Humberside. "Oh no," said Bishop Brunner, "You see four fifths of the Catholics of this Diocese are on Teesside and I think that anybody who is going to succeed as Bishop here, which is what is happening if you are the coadjutor, really needs to know this part of the Diocese first." So I said "Thank you very much for that clarification, where do you want me to go?" "Well, I don't know, I can't think of anywhere," he said. This was all rather frustrating for somebody who had been used to a very business like sort of life. So I said "Is there a convent perhaps?" "Oh no, no convent here," he said, and then after some thought: "Well there is a convent at Whitby, that might do. I'll take you there later and have a look at it." It seemed to be miles from anywhere, that convent. But anyhow he wrote it off when he remembered that Whitby can be cut off in the snow, something I experienced later on.

I left Westminster Cathedral on March 12th 1964 and headed north in the new car which had been presented to me as a leaving gift. I was to journey north with a companion. The previous day the Abbot of Ampleforth, a man called Hume, had called in at the Cathedral and said "I am sure you must feel rather strange about leaving London after twenty-four years here. I am going back to Ampleforth tomorrow and I know you are coming to stay with us for your retreat before consecration, would you like me to drive up with you?" I said "I would be absolutely delighted". That was the beginning of a very close and lasting friendship and I always feel very grateful to him. So he brought me to Ampleforth and there I went into a silent retreat for five or six days.

That was a very strange experience; I felt as though I had died. It wasn't an unhappy feeling at all but it was just that I was emerging into an entirely different life from anything that I had known and it made me feel very isolated. I remember one day going into the Abbey Church, trying to say some prayers and wandering round the different chapels until I came to the Chapel of Our Lady and I asked her to help me to accept this unusual thing that had happened to me and show me how to handle it by her prayers. Then I looked up at the statue, and I absolutely burst into laughter. This is the famous statue, which I hadn't seen before, of Our Lady with a great grin on her face and it looked as if she was really laughing at me for being so ridiculous. This broke the ice for me and I never looked back after that. I laughed aloud all alone in the church.

THE YEARS OF EPISCOPATE

The retreat at Ampleforth marked the end of your 'Years of Priesthood' and the eve of the 'Years of Episcopate'. From there you went directly to Middlesbrough?

Yes. Having completed my stay with the Benedictines I set off for Middlesbrough through that most beautiful drive from Ampleforth via Helmsley to Stokesley right through the dale. I still think it's the pleasantest drive I have ever had; and I've always loved it, scenically and in every other way because it made me feel absolutely full of thanksgiving that my lot was cast in such fair places. It was arranged that I should go and stay, until such a time as any accommodation could be found for me, in the presbytery of St Alphonsus at North Ormesby. The parish priest was Monsignor Alban Nolan, who from the first moment made me feel absolutely at home and whose assistants did likewise and the housekeeper too. They couldn't have been more welcoming. I lived there for some months and I'm ever grateful to them for all they did for me by way of initiating me into the North Yorkshire way of life. Finally they bought a house for me between Middlesbrough and Stokesley, looking onto the Cleveland Hills, which I still miss. It became for me a very lovely home as well as a very interesting apostolate. The other thing that amazed me about the Diocese of Middlesbrough was that it really taught me a lesson. I had thought that one of the most important things in life was efficiency. I had found myself in one of the less well organised dioceses from the administrative point of view. But there was something much better in the place of all that. It was the very loving relationship of the priests with one another, the priests with their Bishop and the Bishop with his priests and it really taught me a lesson that there was something much more important than "Administration".

You arrived in Middlesbrough in the Spring of 1964?

The consecration was on the 19th March, St Joseph's day, in

The old Cathedral Church of St. Mary, Middlesbrough on March 19th, 1964. The consecration of the new Coadjutor Bishop of Middlesbrough.

Enthronement at St. Anne's Cathedral, Leeds on June 27th, 1966. With Mgr. J.J. Kelly, V.G., and Provost Eustace Malone.

*The Bishop Emeritus in his study, 1990.
(Photograph by Jim Moran,
courtesy of 'The Yorkshire Post').*

the old Cathedral. As you can imagine it was a very memorable occasion for me. St Mary's Cathedral was filled to capacity for the event. In the nave were about 120 priests from the Middlesbrough diocese, together with former colleagues from Westminster, representatives of other denominations and civic dignitaries from Teesside and the North and East Ridings. In the sanctuary, I recall, was Abbot Hume, Mgr Casey VG, as well as old friends from Westminster: Monsignor Canon Bartlett, Mgr Row and Fr Kilcoyne. The Bishops of Leeds, and Hexham and Newcastle, and the Auxiliary Bishop of Lancaster were also present in the sanctuary. My co-consecrators were Archbishop Cardinale, Bishop Brunner, and Bishop Craven, the Auxiliary in Westminster. The day was rounded-off by what someone described as a 'regal banquet' at a hotel in Redcar, to which Bishop Brunner had graciously invited some 450 guests. It was a happy start to my new life in the Middlesbrough diocese.

However, you were to spend much of the next two years away from the diocese attending the Second Vatican Council.

Perfectly true. I was really there for too short a time, but I couldn't help that. The Bishop himself had attended the first two sessions of the Council in Rome and when I came along he didn't attend any more. So I was in Rome for a large part of my first two years as a Bishop. I did come back on various occasions and tried my best to tell the clergy of the diocese at different gatherings what I thought was happening. I think they found it very interesting to have a first hand account of the Council.

By the time you became bishop already there had been two sessions of the Council. Had you attended either of those two sessions?

On a previous visit to Rome I had on one occasion been in for a short time just as an ordinary Priest whilst I was still Administrator of Westminster Cathedral. However I was a Council Father for the last two sessions, under the Pontificate of Paul VI. Whilst some of the greatest battles had been fought in the earlier sessions only one Constitution and one Decree had been promulgated by that stage. Therefore at least another 14 had yet to be debated, voted upon and ratified when I went to Rome in the autumn of 1964. Indeed there were on-going arguments well into the final session. I found the Council one of the greatest experiences of my life, as you can imagine. Every day's session began with a Mass, different liturgies, different rites, Latin and Oriental, and altogether it was a wonderful spiritual experience. We always attended in full choir dress. This in a sense emphasised the fact that we were taking part in something more than an ordinary conference. The east window in St Peter's beyond the Papal altar, with its representation of the Holy Spirit in the form of a dove, was a constant reminder of the need to listen and to learn in humility and love.

During the Council most English and Welsh bishops stayed at the Venerable English College of which many of them were alumni. I resided in the new Beda college opposite the Basilica of St Paul's Outside the Walls, together with Archbishop Cowderoy of Southwark, Bishop Cunningham of Hexham and Newcastle, Bishop Wall of Brentwood and Bishop Grant of Northampton. Bishop Cunningham always referred to me during this period as 'Teudali' (the Titular See to which I was appointed in 1964). "What does Teudali think about this?" he would say when we were discussing an issue. The Council was a great social and informative experience because one got to know Bishops from all parts of the world. One didn't only meet them in the Council Chamber, but on innumerable other occasions. Bishops sat in the Vatican Council in order of the date of their consecration. So at first I was almost out on the piazza. There was, however, a very good loud speaker system which was highly desirable because all the sessions were in Latin. There was only one great person who ever spoke in any other language, as far as I can remember, and that was Maximus IV, the Patriarch of Antioch, who insisted the church wasn't entirely a Latin church and spoke in French. But, everyone else had to give their speeches in Latin. You had ten minutes for your speech. If you exceeded the ten minutes you were gonged. There were four Moderators, all Cardinals, who took the chair in turn at each of the sessions which started from early in the morning, until lunchtime. The other events took place in the late afternoon and the evening. The Secretary of the Council, Archbishop Felice, who was a very fluent Latin speaker, spoke so clearly in Latin that it was perfectly easy to understand everything he was saying. It wasn't always easy to understand what everyone else was saying, especially for example the Spanish; we found it very difficult to understand Spanish Latin because of the lisp.

During the third session of the Council I made a written submission on social justice and the distribution of material wealth. In the following year, 1965, I gave two speeches in the course of the fourth session. On one occasion I spoke about the problems of the Third World and on another, along with Bishops Butler and Grant, I intervened during the debate on nuclear weapons. When I made the second speech I remember I was gonged just as I got to the end of my script but I was allowed one more sentence to finish it off, which I did. The Moderator on that occasion was Cardinal Suenens whom I got to know very well later on. He came and stayed with me at Bishop's House. I enjoyed reminding him that he gonged me in the Council. But one of the more interesting gonging experiences was of some old Cardinal who went on and on and on even after he had been gonged twice and eventually the Moderator said "Reverendissime et Eminentissime Principe, tempus exhaustum est et nos exhausti sumus!" - "time's up and we're worn out too".

My memories of the Council are of a very enriching experience and I always defend the Council, as the twenty first General Council of the Church. The thing I always point out to people is that it could only have happened because of the twenty that preceded it. I suppose this is the historical approach but it is nevertheless valid. Vatican II couldn't have happened without Vatican I, which couldn't have happened without Trent which couldn't have happened without Florence and so on right back to the great Councils of the early Church, the Christological ones. So the Council is part of the 'development of doctrine', the exposition of the teachings of Christ, as He promised would happen throughout the ages. Moreover, it is never fair to judge the Second Vatican Council by the aberrations that followed it.

These aberrations were due to a complete misunderstanding on the part of a great many priests and others of what had really happened in the Council. The answer is to study the Decrees. Bishops from all over the world had been together for four years and had been enriched by a greater vision of the unity, holiness, universality and apostolicity of the Church. They couldn't quickly pass this on to others. Most of us certainly tried to do everything possible to help the clergy, in the first instance, to understand what had really happened in the Council. Nevertheless, it quickly became clear that this would take years rather than months or weeks or days. So, things that happened afterwards, departing from the permanent tradition of the Church were perhaps excusable in the sense that it was very hard for people to weigh up exactly what had happened. Indeed one is told historically that similar situations have arisen after every General Council with sad consequences. After 1870, for example, the Old Catholics withdrew, but the Church of God sails on. I always defend the Second Vatican Council and point out its many fruits throughout the world. The implementation of its Decrees still continues because people haven't absorbed the reality of what God was saying to us all.

You have spoken elsewhere of Cardinal Newman as the 'Hidden Presence' at the Second Vatican Council. Perhaps you could explain what you mean by that?

Although the name of Newman does not often appear in the Council's interventions, the entire ethos which one finds there bespeaks the kind of approach to a whole range of matters that was his. This has a lot to do with the lucidity of his thought, and the perfection of its expression, encapsulated at home, and even more so abroad, in his literary clarity This has had a profound impact on all philosophical and theological studies in the modern era. In the Council one became aware of the international knowledge of the life and work and inspiration of the man.

It is difficult to imagine how a great deal of the Council's thinking on the Church, Revelation, Conscience, and the participation of the laity could have been formulated apart from the intellectual groundwork done by Newman in the nineteenth century. It would have been difficult for the ecclesiology of *Lumen Gentium* to have emerged without *The Development of Doctrine*. Indeed, at one point in the Council Cardinal Gracias suggested that this work of Newman's ought to be the trail whereby Vatican II should proceed. In a sense it was. The constitution on Divine Revelation drew heavily on Newman's insight on scripture and tradition. The Decrees on the Laity, on Ecumenism, Christian Education, and the Declaration on Religious Liberty, together with some aspects of *Gaudium et Spes*, all bear the hallmark of his thought and influence. So much so that he is thought of as a Doctor of the twentieth century even more than the nineteenth: a man in advance of his time.

But there is more to Newman than his intellectual endowments, for he had the mark of sanctity. His spirituality, his life of incessant prayer, total dedication, absolute honesty and absolute humility bespeaks the Saint. He showed people of our times how to live a deeply Christian life in the midst of indifference and all the hostile influences of today. I have a feeling that this century, which has known the fullness of his light, will not end before he is raised to the altars of the Church. For this many of us work and pray, confident that, by God's grace, it will happen eventually.

You returned to Middlesbrough from the fourth and final session of the Council just before Christmas 1965. But even then you did not have very much time to exercise your ministry in the diocese because six months later you were appointed Bishop of Leeds.

This all arose because in the previous year Archbishop Grimshaw of Birmingham had died and he had been succeeded in the Autumn of 1965 by the then Bishop of Leeds, George Patrick Dwyer. The Holy See had, therefore, to fill the Diocese of Leeds. I can remember to my surprise being told by the Apostolic Delegate, (the same Archbishop Cardinale who had consecrated me as Bishop in Middlesbrough) that the Holy See was in a dilemma about whom it should appoint to Leeds and thought that although I had only been a short time in Middlesbrough, I had already had some experience of Yorkshire and it would be good if I took over. Well I wasn't very enthusiastic about this but I said "Again I must say to you that I will do what the Holy See wants me to do." So that is how it happened and I can remember the day that I was enthroned as Bishop of Leeds, feeling quite ill and very sad at leaving the lovely North Riding and the Diocese of Middlesbrough. Of course, I soon found that there was an excellent spirit also in the Diocese of Leeds, in which I had a very warm welcome.

Presumably you went to Leeds with a single objective in mind which was to implement the Council?

Exactly. Paul VI gave each of us in the Council a simple gold ring thought to be symbolic of our role, and a beautifully illuminated book on the life of St Charles Borromeo. We wondered why he had given us the latter until he said "St Charles Borromeo, Archbishop of Milan, was the Bishop who in the 16th century best implemented the decrees of the Council of Trent. Now you go back to your own Diocese and implement in a balanced manner the decrees of the Second Vatican Council." And so with a challenge like that one felt that at once one must get to work on it. That is why I thought of founding a Pastoral and Ecumenical Centre in the Diocese of Leeds so that there could be dialogue with the clergy and the people which would convey to them the meaning of the decrees of the Second Vatican Council.

My feeling in 1966 was that the enrichment shared by those of us who had been present at the Council itself had not, as yet, really percolated through to either our clergy or the laity. This was understandable, but I wanted to ensure that the spirit of renewal was communicated to all our people. This was one of the main reasons for the foundation, in 1967, of Wood Hall as a Pastoral and Ecumenical Centre for the Leeds diocese; it was, of course, the first one of its kind in the country.

Can you explain how Wood Hall was meant to assist in the implementation of Vatican II?

My first aim was as far as possible to do everything to enable the clergy, who were going to lead the people in the parishes, to enter more fully into the spirit of Vatican II. That spirit is the working out of what Newman called the 'Development of Doctrine' which is all very clearly expressed by Our Lord, Himself, in the Scriptures when He says that "There are many things that you must hear but you cannot hear them now but when He the Spirit of Truth has come to you all these things will be revealed". In the early life of the Church the first Great General Councils dealt with Christology: with the real meaning of the Incarnation and all its different aspects. Later other matters emerged from a deeper study of the Scriptures which has led to a great unfolding of God's revelation for the world through all the ages. So it was very important to have study groups for the priests not only in the immediate aftermath of the Council but also as an on-going thing. This applied to Bishops also, and they have frequently got together to study the implementation of the decrees. That was very largely for the benefit of those who had not had the initial experience of being at the Council.

We did everything we could in our different ways to help our priests. With hindsight I would like to have put much more into this than we actually did. We might then have avoided some of the greater problems that later arose. At any rate, I did set out to bring the spirit of Vatican II to the clergy in innumerable courses which we laid on not only at Wood Hall but at Hazlewood and at Ilkley and then at the UNI which was established at Upholland, and through many other channels. It was hoped that this would lead to courses for the laity on the parish level, but it is clear that that was expecting a great deal in a short time.

How far clergy and people benefited from this process one cannot say; it has not taken place as completely as it should have done and one sometimes examines one's conscience as to what more could have been done. There is, however, a great wisdom in everything connected with God's Church. She moves very slowly and very gently to enable her to carry the people of God along with her. So, by God's grace it is still happening and it is gradually enriching the life of individuals and of parishes. It has had its unfortunate effects as well. It has led some people to believe that they have lost the traditions in which they were first brought up. This was never intended by the Church.

The Second Vatican Council itself clung to the great and fundamental traditions of the Church's life: the wisdom of all the ages. It would be very wrong for both bishops and priests to mislead their people in their understanding of the Council. The Council was meant to be a great pastoral council. It was meant to be a great spiritual renewal. That was the idea of John XXIII. It was to be a great retreat for the whole world; but he would have been aghast if he had lived to see some of the things that have happened. Some people today are still aghast at aspects which are not true to the mind of the Church. One could give many illustrations such as the minimising of the importance of regular Confession. Every Bishop in the Council would have been outraged at such happenings.

I have always gone out of my way to defend the Second Vatican Council but never its aberrations and it seems to me that this is a very vital matter. To measure it historically as well as theologically is essential. So, I would say that there is still very considerable work to be done concerning the implementation of the Council. And it can only be done correctly under the aegis and guidance of the successors of St Peter and the Apostles in union with the Sensus Fidelium of the whole People of God in Truth and in Love. One regrets the lack of progress that has been made in following and carrying out the Council. One thanks God for the good things that have happened. One has been bitterly disappointed by some of the sad things that have happened: the defection of some clergy and Religious and some of the bizarre ideas that have been put forward, quite wrongly, as a part of the package of Vatican II.

> *One of the other innovations with which you are credited is the creation of the first Diocesan Pastoral Council following Vatican II.*

That is quite true. The Pastoral Council was very much something emanating from the existence of Wood Hall. Monsignor Michael Buckley was the first warden of Wood Hall. He was there for the first 10 years of its existence and it's important to recognise his contribution to its work. In 1970, for example, Wood Hall hosted the first national gathering of priests, which had been convened by the hierarchy of England and Wales. That was the beginning of the event which now takes place every year in Newman College, Birmingham. Similarly, almost from the start we had a Council of the Laity. These two entities of Priests and People ultimately led to the Pastoral Council. Now looking back on this I think perhaps our strategy in the first instance was wrong because we set up the top layer of the structure before we had founded the fundamental ones that had to support it. The most fundamental one of all being the parish community. Whilst from the start I tried to encourage priests to establish Parish Councils which could feed in to the wider community of Deanery and Diocese, it was never sufficiently general to be effective. The failure of a very large number of places to establish their parish councils or committees, had its effect on the real validity of the larger entities. With this hindsight I would want to have begun with a patient but insistent creation of a parish community in each place. When this had become a community of the whole parish, with dialogue between the priests, Religious and all the people, praying together, studying together, learning together, and working together, then we would have had a more solid basis for going forward to other levels in the structure. Fortunately today it seems to me to be very well on the way to fulfilment. People have realised more and more that if they have not got these primary structures in place they are going to be deprived of a richness which ought to be theirs.

Earlier, you described Wood Hall as a Pastoral and Ecumenical Centre. Perhaps you could tell us something about the second aspect, and about ecumenism generally following Vatican II?

Yes. Although the pastoral application of the Council was important, so too was the Ecumenical one. For us this was something new as it was really the first time that the Catholic Church had committed itself to this phenomenon which had been going on in the non-Catholic churches for most of this century. We came to the Ecumenical situation perhaps more mature in one sense than those who had started it because we had had time to weigh up the pros and cons of it in so many different ways. But it was a break-through from the point of view of immediate, much closer relationships with all the non-Catholic bodies.

This had been greatly inspired in our country by a conference held at Heythrop in Oxfordshire in 1962 at which Cardinal Bea was present. (He was a Jesuit appointed by Pope John XXIII to be the first head of the secretariat for Christian Unity.) I gave a paper on that occasion. Cardinal Bea had made us realise that the essential principles underlying genuine Ecumenism were to be those found in the fourth chapter of the Epistle to the Ephesians in which St Paul speaks of "Our growing up together in Christ, in truth and in love - *in veritate et in caritate*". That, incidentally, was why I chose those two words when I had to have my coat of arms granted as a Bishop: ***Veritas et Caritas*** "Truth and Love". And Cardinal Bea emphasised that the two must always go together. It is no use having love without truth, he said, or truth without love, because truth without love can become intolerance and love without truth can become sentimentality. There was one other very special thing that Cardinal Bea had said: "Don't forget that ecumenism is always going to bear the sign of the Cross. There is always going to be a Calvary on the way to this resurrection".

You have got to have the two together and this was very well illustrated for me by the representative of the Archbishop of Canterbury, Bishop Moorman from Ripon. He had said once in a discourse: "Imagine a field in which there is a crucifix at the far end of the field and all God's people, all the followers of Christ are gathered at the other end of the field. As they advance towards the Crucifix, they are closer and closer to one another." They are rubbing shoulders with one another. This focus on the person of Christ Our Lord who is 'The Truth' is perhaps the most important consideration in ecumenism. It is not only the most important, but it emphasises the fact that you must have the truth about whom Christ is. And you must have the love that Christ shows. This has always been for me the key to true ecumenism. Many people get it all wrong. They think that ecumenism means that you have got to get the lowest common multiple or a highest common factor of doctrine. It isn't that at all. It is that we have got all, in the first instance, to become better Catholics, better Anglicans, better Methodists, better Quakers and so on. It is only when we grow to be more Christ-like that the right sort of ecumenism is going to develop.

The Decree of the Second Vatican Council on Ecumenism makes it quite explicit that there is no confrontation or disharmony between the reception of converts into the fullness of faith, and at the same time the progress of ecumenism. Some people have been stopped from embracing the fullness of faith, thinking that it is unecumenical to do so. The two can go side by side, however, because the whole question of conscience makes it absolutely certain that when you know a greater fullness, you must be free to embrace it. So there is no incompatibility at all between working for the unity of Christendom and at the same time embracing the fullness of faith when this is recognised.

Now, you may ask, how far the sort of ecumenical relationship I described earlier has happened? I think it has happened in a very remarkable manner. For example, when we opened Wood Hall, there were representatives of the other churches there, including the Bishop of Ripon. Archbishop Cardinale the Apostolic Delegate came to open it and from the start we had all sorts of sessions, with very distinguished people like Cardinal Gray from Scotland, the Archbishop of York and a great variety of other participants. An on-going study of *veritas et caritas* took place and I like to think that at Wood Hall for the most part we adhered to those truths.

I have felt throughout that it has been absolutely essential that we do not diminish one iota of fundamental Catholic teaching in our attitude to ecumenism. And I think that it is fair to say that we credited others with the same kind of approach. Humanly speaking it is always difficult to see how unity can happen. In the providence of God, however, it could be brought about, though only by His grace. As the great Abbe Coutourier said: "It can only happen in the way that He wills and at the time that He wills". Therefore I never had any patience with people who said: "Oh we must have a target for achieving unity in this year or that." That is not the way that God works. It is a sort of Pelagianism suggesting you can do everything yourself. We know, however, that without Christ we can do nothing. This has been the spirit of our ecumenism and whenever I saw it diverting from the principles laid down regarding our relationships with one another, I tried to make it quite clear that this was not the way indicated by the Council. It is absolutely essential in the pagan world of our time that there should be a common Christian front. That can only come, however, from the sincere working together of the whole People of God in truth and love. This calls for patience and prayer. By and large there has been a good adherence to the fundamental principles, and things have only gone haywire where they have not been observed. A very obvious example of this is the question of intercommunion. There have been some people who think that intercommunion is the quick way to unity. This is not the purpose of Holy Communion. It is for God to decide when His unity - the unity for which we pray, and the unity for which we work, shall happen. Intercommunion is the crown of unity achieved and far from being the means to that end it could frustrate that organic unity intended by the Church.

> *In the aftermath of Vatican II a growing number of men left the priesthood. For someone in your position during these years this phenomenon must have been a cause for great sadness?*

Oh it was a terrible sadness. I think in a sense that the period covered by my years of Episcopacy, must have been one of the most distressing in the life of the Church. It certainly caused very great sorrow to Bishops who couldn't understand why this was happening. I still don't know why it happened. It is a complete misunderstanding of Vatican II to say that the Council was responsible. The Council wasn't responsible. It was something quite different and relates to contemporary secular society as well. This was the age of the permissive society. The whole of society was involved in this matter. It was something, to my mind, which was part of a sociological phenomenon.

So you think it would have happened anyway because of the social climate in the 1960's?

Yes, but we must be careful not to exaggerate this. While the defections were very shocking they were relatively few when you consider the great number who stayed who also had to cope with a new vision of Church and did so very admirably. It was very distressing to see people whom one valued greatly get hold of the wrong end of the stick. They associated their position with something that was happening in the Church when it was something that was happening in the world. I'm still not really able to explain the defections, and although the numbers were not very great they were far too many. One has got to remember, however, that in the past such defections usually took place without publicity. They were always a very great sorrow to a Bishop and often he was the only person that really knew about them. The frailty of human nature should never surprise us. Grace can elevate but never destroy nature. In the 1960s and 70s the scandal caused by priestly defection was intensified by the fact that whereas in the past publicity was rare, in that period the mass media was obsessed with the subject because it was always linked to the question of celibacy. But I remember somebody saying to me "Provided it hits the headlines, it's all right; it's when it turns to one small paragraph on the back page that you should be worried about it" and there's a lot in that.

Because the vast majority of such defections were concerned with a desire to marry, Paul VI's approach was to grant the dispensation from celibacy when requested in order to enable the people concerned to be validly married and to live a Catholic life and receive the sacraments. This had a difficult consequence in one sense because lay people very understandably asked why couldn't they be dispensed more easily from the very solemn vows made in marriage, which surely are no less solemn than the vows of celibacy? It seemed as though defecting priests were being dispensed far too easily. Moreover after it had been going on some time, the Church began to feel very unhappy about the expedience of this solution because there were already many cases of priests wanting to break-up what had been ill-considered unions and in some cases to return to their original status.

So it became very clear that somehow or other there must be a tightening up. Pope Paul VI suffered agonies about it all and it was very important therefore that those who succeeded him should tighten up this whole matter and that is where things have remained. Perhaps it's now gone to the other extreme: but it is very difficult to get the balance. By and large, thank God, most of the priests of every Diocese were loyal to the life of the Church and to the Laws of God and to the promises they made and one hopes that the 'silly season' so to speak is over in that matter. But there will always be some defections as there were in the past.

> *Another feature of the post-Concilar period in this country has been the decline in vocations to the priesthood. Are the consequences of this trend entirely detrimental to the life of the Church?*

That's not a very easy to question to answer but let me say that in our part of the Western World we have suffered far less than most countries. The numbers of vocations were slightly reduced for a few years. We were no longer getting vocations, or very few, straight from the schools into the secular priesthood; but we were getting a lot more mature people and this in a sense was a great advantage. Of course, we can always hope for an increase of vocations and for this we constantly work and pray. It is important also to face the future realistically. Nevertheless we can never qualify the work of the Holy Spirit. This makes it all an entirely different matter than prognostications in industry. And who knows but what, in the next few years, there might be some great resurgence of vocations?

Moreover in other parts of the world, especially behind the Iron Curtain, there is such a glut of vocations that they just can't accept them all, and this is true in Africa and in the Southern Hemisphere generally. There was an old saying "God gives people the priests they deserve" and I believe that will always happen.

> *At the end of the day what is the essential role of the priest in the Catholic community? What is it that makes the priest indispensable?*

The Mass, the Holy Mass. This is the thing that really makes him indispensable. The Mass is an act of Christ, of Christ the great High Priest: it is also the act of the priest who, by the Sacrament of Holy Order, shares in a special way in the High Priesthood of Christ. That is why we should venerate and love the priesthood. For this is the office of men chosen by God and set apart to perform with him the sacrifice. In a way that is unique, Christ the Priest is Christ the Shepherd. The priesthood is a loving service because it is an identification with the Good Shepherd who gave his life for his sheep. It is necessarily therefore a life of sacrifice, coupled with the joy which comes from the Resurrection. Priestly service is the call to be as Christ: all things to all men. It gives a new dimension to all earthly forms of service, which in the priesthood are sacramentalized and exercised on a plane that is different from all else. Priestly joy and priestly identity may be found only in that happy sacrifice which is shared with Christ the great High Priest of all the human race.

> *If Catholic priests have abandoned their ministry in the past because of celibacy and we accept that this is also one reason for the decline in the number of ordinations that obviously raises the question of a married priesthood. Is this something that you would favour?*

When I was an Anglican clergyman I was always looking out for the right wife. When I became a Catholic, however, I became very aware of the apostolic value of celibacy, in that the priest is set free to be the Father of all his people. Of course nowadays some would say this is a very paternalistic attitude. I realise that, but even if you don't talk about it from the paternal point of view you can talk about it as a loving service wherein the priest is somebody who belongs to every family and none in particular. Take the case of an Anglican clergyman: suppose I had got married, suppose my wife had presented me with sons and daughters. When I was offered preferment which would enable me to do more for my family would I be wrong to put that as a priority? Surely it is possible to think the natural law would indicate that acceptance of a better living might have family advantages however dedicated I was to my present assignment. I would want to do more for the education of my own family, and to help them in all sorts of ways. Now as a priest one has no need to do that. The Catholic priest knows that he is free to do, as we understand it, what God wants him to do: to stay where he is if

God wants him to stay, or for the same reason to move elsewhere. By God's Grace I would say that celibacy is the ideal. Of course there will always be scandals. A priest is a man and God has built his priesthood on manhood. It is however a manhood that is engraced in a special way: not by way of destruction but by gradual transformation tempered by humility and love.

A related issue, of course, is the ordination of women to the priesthood. What are your views on this question?

When God took on our human nature for our salvation and sanctification He deliberately chose to become man. At the same time He paid the highest tribute to womanhood in choosing and preparing the Blessed Virgin Mary as the vehicle of the birth of His Son and her son. In her womb the Eternal priest was formed. When on the night of the Last Supper, the eve of His crucifixion, He ordained His Apostles to share in His High Priesthood, it was an entirely masculine event because the actions they and their successors were to perform involved a total identification with Himself. They were to act in His Person, unworthy as they might be. The Catholic Priesthood from the start, in this identification with the manhood of Christ, was something entirely different from ministry. And the fact that Our Lord, had in His own mission 'liberated' women to assist Him fully in all sorts of ways short of raising a single one - not even His own Blessed Mother - to Priesthood, bears eloquent testimony - as does their absence from the first Ordination and all subsequent ones in the life of God's Church - that womanhood has an entirely different role to play but one of inestimable worth - which is unobtainable by manhood. This is the tradition of all the ages until the end of time.

I always remember Bishop Winnington Ingram of London in the thirties holding a conference on women priests. Among those present was Prebendary McKay, the High Church Vicar of All Saints, Margaret Street, and a person who held entirely 'Catholic' views. He never opened his mouth at this discussion, so eventually Dr Winnington Ingram said "I'm sure it would be a help to know what Prebendary McKay thinks about this situation." So Prebendary McKay with an absolute poker face got up and said "Well, My Lord, I would like just to ask a question. If the Archbishop of York became betrothed to the Archbishop of

Canterbury in which See would she reside after the Marriage?" The possibility of raising women to the Priesthood in the Church of England has sadly become an obstacle to ecclesial unity.

In one sense you broke the tradition regarding Holy Orders when you became the first bishop in this country to ordain married deacons. What prompted this move?

It came about because the Council put forward the idea of the Permanent Diaconate, in contrast to its simply being one step on the way to Priesthood. Theologically the Diaconate is part of the sacrament of Holy Order which comprises Bishops, Priests and Deacons going right back to scriptural times, to the Acts of the Apostles. In the remote past many ordained people would remain as deacons and this was not confined to the unmarried. Vatican II recommended the restoration of the Permanent Diaconate, married or unmarried, decreeing in the former case the agreement of the wife. At the time we implemented this, one of the chief advantages of a Deacon was that, apart from the Priest, he was the only one who could distribute Holy Communion. He could go to the Tabernacle and take the Blessed Sacrament out. He couldn't, of course, say Mass because that's for the priesthood. This appealed to many of the clergy even the most conservative ones. It offered the prospect of having somebody else to help them in the distribution of Holy Communion and so the married diaconate became very attractive from that point of view. But that was a very limited point of view and therefore an unbalanced one as we discovered very quickly afterwards when the Pope gave permission for those raised to the Ministry of Acolyte to distribute Holy Communion. And then only a few months after that came the very wide decree which enabled both ordinary men and women to assist in Holy Communion where there was a pastoral need, and led to the widespread introduction into parish life of Eucharistic Ministers. Their ministry represents a great enrichment of the whole life of the Church in many ways. Let me give you an example: it quite often happens that there are elderly people who have been daily communicants all through life, but are now sick and ill, or house-bound. Yes, the local Priest can come a certain number of times to bring them Holy Communion, perhaps weekly, perhaps monthly. Now with this wonderful concession of Eucharistic Ministers such people can receive Holy Communion every day if they want to do so. It has been a great deprivation for them after being daily communicants all their lives not to have the Blessed Sacrament frequently in their declining years when more than ever they want to be drawing closer to God. Of course, some people in the first instance said "Oh, I think I'd rather go without Holy Communion than have it from a man or a woman." I've always answered them by saying "May I tell you something? If I was in your condition and I were in my own home and I couldn't have anyone to bring me Holy Communion every day unless it was a lay-person, I wouldn't mind who it was that brought it to me as long as it was according to the mind of the Church. Anyone who brought me My Lord and Saviour would be more than welcome."

The presence in our parishes today of Eucharistic Ministers emphasises the point that the Diaconate is not only about giving Holy Communion. It has an important role to fill in the whole of the Church's life. For example, a Deacon is allowed to preach. Anyone who is allowed to preach in the Catholic Church must have considerable training in Theology, both dogmatic and moral; and this has not always been done in the preparation of the married deacons. We did our best to see that it was done here and our Deacons were given a very full course of instruction. If they have this they can be very important in the whole of evangelisation. The Diaconate also is a part of the sacrament of Holy Order from the Catholic point of view.

Does the decline in priestly vocations reflect badly on the Catholic school system?

Very much so because in the post-conciliar period many schools quite wrongly set aside the whole of the old system of teaching catechetics without having decided upon a satisfactory alternative. This wasn't primarily the fault of the teachers. It was just a very unfortunate happening on the part of their mentors at that time. They were radical, they must approach the whole thing in a new way and so, for example, they threw out the old 'penny catechism' and in a sense never put anything in its place. Therefore in religious instruction in the schools you got some very interesting excursions into the mission field or nature study and into the needs of the Third World but no real knowledge of God, of the meaning of life, the meaning of prayer, the meaning of worship, the meaning of the seven sacraments and so forth. The

Holy See has been trying ever since to do its utmost to see that in all the countries of the world there is a return to a properly constructed system of catechetics. This is still in the process of production though of course in latter years there have been some very good developments which have brought us nearer to what is required. This is not totally true by any means and it was very rash to disregard what had worked very well for many generations before finding something that was going to take its place. Moreover, even in the latest papal documents it has been made quite clear that this modern fashion in education of despising the faculty of memory is highly regrettable; after all it is one of the three faculties of the soul.

Maybe the catechism answers were beyond the intellectual apprehension of many of those who learnt them at the time but they were fixed in their minds and when in later life they were asked questions they always were able to give an answer even if it was the old catechism answer that was embedded in their memory. G.K. Chesterton for one appreciated that little book. It was a very deplorable lack of balance that destroyed the whole of that system. So much so that Cardinal Heenan produced a new edition of the 'penny catechism', (which then became the sixpenny catechism), but it came too late.

The Catholic community in England and Wales has expended a great deal of money on its schools over the years. Should it continue to do to do so in the future?

I have no hesitation in saying yes to that question. When I became a Bishop I found a very great difference between a parish that had a Catholic school, - and by that I generally mean a Catholic primary school - and those who hadn't. There was a whole difference in ethos. There was a gap, a lacuna in those places where there was not a Catholic primary school. About the Catholic secondary school - I find it difficult to give quite so strong an answer. But this is only my own experience. The Church maintains that children ought to have the advantage of a Catholic school throughout the period of their education. I would go along with that and say that it should be on the consciences of parents who don't send their children to a Catholic school where there is one that is adequate from every point of view.

In some areas at present the middle schools are being abolished and they are going back to the extended primary school. This is highly acceptable to the parish clergy for the longer they can keep children in the sphere of the parish, the greater their contribution to total community. In their day the Catholic grammar schools did a great work. Many of the Catholic public schools likewise have performed in a highly dedicated manner both academically and from the religious point of view. Nevertheless it is quite true that schools of all kinds go through different phases. A first class school is almost always the product of a dedicated and talented Headteacher and staff. The staff are vitally important in any school: so important that they can determine the whole atmosphere of the place. There is everything to be said for the Catholic school when it has got a really dedicated Catholic staff because to teach is a high vocation in the eyes of the Church. So one would hope that our schools will always play their full role in the Catholic community.

On the other hand there are people who think that in later stages, just as a university has got a number of different faiths, that in the sixth forms or maybe even before that, there ought to be some give and take. I would say that provided there was a school that was good from the Catholic point of view as well as from the secular point of view then everybody ought to make it their choice. But it isn't always like that. I had an interesting experience when I was a young priest at Westminster Cathedral when I was asked to see a group of Catholic boys who were at Westminster public school, near the Abbey. When they came to see me they were quite avid to know the answers to historical questions regarding the Church for they were very anxious to be able to defend their faith in the history classes and this was a very good challenge to them. So there were some advantages of being a Catholic in a non-Catholic school, because they had the courage to hold their own. But it's not every group of boys, I suppose, that would have that courage. Even the older ones often need the support of a school which has an avowedly Catholic ethos.

> *Perhaps we could look at the four key documents which were produced by Vatican II, the four constitutions which have shaped Catholic teaching in recent years. There was the document on the Church in the Modern World, the one on the Church as the People of God, the one on Liturgy and the final docu-*

ment on Divine Revelation. Which of these do you feel has had the greatest impact?

The one you mentioned second is the one I would always put first - *Lumen Gentium* - the Great Constitution on the Church. Whilst many people think of it as putting forward solely the idea of the Church in the terminology of the 'People of God' in actuality it incorporates a complete ecclesiology and indeed Mariology which has been a tremendous enrichment to the life of the whole body. The Bishop of Ripon, who was the Archbishop of Canterbury's representative at the Second Vatican Council, thought that the Constitution on Scripture and Tradition was the most important one ecumenically synthesising as it did these two elements. That was indeed a vitally important document. The one, however, that had the biggest impact on the people, of course, was the Liturgical one. At the Council, the Liturgy Decree was the first important one to be approved and so had priority of implementation, so to speak. But it should be remembered that when the Council discussed the Church's liturgy the issue of the vernacular hardly ever came into it at all. The great plea on the vernacular came from behind the Iron Curtain where the only opportunity for catechesis was in the Mass. That was the great argument for the vernacular but the vernacular is scarcely mentioned in the Decree itself. The main theme of the Decree is 'participation' and one has got to remember that there was already considerable participation in the Latin Mass. Assisted greatly by parallel missals in Latin and English, for example, participation of the people in 'Dialogue Masses' had developed far more than is remembered today. The International Liturgical Movement had really prepared the way for the Liturgical Decree. And most of its thinking ultimately appeared in the new Missal of Paul VI which is, of course, written in Latin.

In each country the Bishops had to implement this Decree and very quickly. The vernacular came to be a priority question since it was thought to enable a greater participation. The Sacred Congregation in Rome gave more and more concessions. Looking back on this, I can see the providence of God in it: for the Church isn't just a Latin church, it is a Universal Church and in a sense the Latin doesn't necessarily express Universality, though it did and still does for many people. Universality, however, has got to include languages that have no Latin roots whatsoever; it's only the European languages, generally speaking that derive from Latin roots. But, whilst one may be able to see the providence of God in what has happened, it certainly wasn't meant to be implemented so swiftly. In fact it needed much greater catechesis.

In our own hierarchy, I had been working for years with Archbishop Grimshaw and Bishop Dwyer on liturgical studies. Together with other English speaking countries, we formed a 'caucus' concerned with liturgical reform whilst still at the Council. When the question of the vernacular arose I tried to put forward the idea that any vernacular translation should be done as ecumenically as possible. Therefore there was a lot to be said for the 'prayer book' form of language - the 'thee' and the 'thou'. There were long debates about this and, of course, ultimately it was defeated. I defended it up to the hilt. Looking back I think perhaps I did so quite wrongly because I didn't realise at the time that the Anglicans were already opting for a more modern style of language. There are those who think that in so doing we have both lost something of the dignity of worship.

On the English scene when Archbishop Dwyer's term as Chairman of the National Liturgical Commission came to an end, I was asked to take over the Chair which I did for the next five years and that was a period of considerable interest and development. As you can imagine, for me personally the liturgical reforms went against the grain, and were one of the hardest things I have had to do: returning to the vernacular after saying Mass for more than a quarter of a century in Latin. I suppose that it was more of a shock for me to return to the vernacular than to people who had only known Latin all their lives. Latin was understandably for me a symbol of the gift of the fullness of Faith. Nevertheless the Mass is the Mass in whatever language it is said.

Amongst other things, the Chairman of the National Commission on Liturgy in our country is *ipso facto* the representative on ICEL which is the body concerned with the implementation of the Liturgical Decree in the English speaking world and especially in the question of translation. It is based in Washington DC and has a difficult role to fulfil if it is going to satisfy all English speaking nations with a universal standard form of vernacular translation. American English and Australian English and South African English are very different from English

English and with all the dialogue in the world it is very difficult always to get a consensus.

Before it became clear that the Holy See wanted a common vernacular translation for each international language group, we in England went ahead with a vernacular Missal of our own which was published by Goodliffe Neale. This is almost forgotten to-day. But there are few who would deny that it is a much more apt translation, at least for England and Wales, than the one produced shortly afterwards by ICEL.

You will realise from what I have already said that I was never fully happy about the ICEL translation. And I feel that the only good thing I managed to get through when I was on ICEL was to see that they set up an on-going commission for an ultimate revision. This is now being done and some very plausible results are emerging from real consultation. But during my term of office I had some very considerable arguments with my colleagues. For example they put forward a translation for the Form of Confirmation. To my mind it wasn't a translation of the Latin at all, yet nobody seemed to be bothered about it except me. So I took it to Rome to the Sacred Congregation. They didn't seem to be very interested in it either. So when I had my private audience with Paul VI I put it before him and I remember his bursting into Latin and saying "This is indeed an incorrect translation of the Latin form". Subsequently His Holiness sent an order to the Congregation to suppress it and in the future never to give permission for any translation of the form of a Sacrament, in any language, without it being referred personally to him. This made me the most unpopular Bishop in the world with the Sacred Congregation, for a time at least!

> *The other major liturgical change which people associate with the period after the Vatican Council is 'Mass facing the people'. To some extent this was happening before the Vatican Council but it has become almost universal now. Was this something that was envisaged at the time?*

No, not in the way that it has taken place. It all goes back to the fact that in the Roman Basilicas, whenever the Popes celebrated Mass they did so 'facing the people' but it was the unique prerogative of the Pope. The decree makes it quite clear that the

Liturgy of the Word should be said facing the people. It also lays down that newly constructed fixed altars should enable the Priest to face the people for the Eucharistic Liturgy. The reordering of existing sanctuaries must always be done with great sensitivity. Sometimes this demands that the Eucharistic part of the Holy Sacrifice be said in the more traditional manner. Rome quickly realised the sort of vandalism that could happen and indeed did happen. People started playing about with very historic and wonderful buildings and shocking depredations have taken place. Such happenings were never intended and should never occur. Others have resorted to the solution of portable wooden altars - which is against all liturgical tradition. Sanctuaries should never be cluttered up with two altars.

> *One of the unfortunate consequences of the changes of the 1960s has been the damage done to some of our churches and the loss of historic features in many of those churches in the cause of alleged improvements. But reform went further than that didn't it?*

The same thing applies, of course, to the abolition of popular devotions. It is often forgotten, however, that these things began to happen long before the Council. It was Pope Pius XII, for example, who by radically mitigating the Eucharistic fast, made evening Masses a feature of all our lives and one which to some extent displaced the traditional kind of evening services. Nowadays nobody will regret this great concession but the Church is only beginning to realise that she suffers from this depletion of other aspects of her life. However, there is now a healthy sign, thanks especially to Pope John Paul II, of the revival of traditional devotions to the Blessed Sacrament and Our Lady and the Saints.

> *Some people would argue that being a Catholic has become easier since the Vatican Council. In some superficial ways perhaps that's true given the advent of, for example, vigil Masses, the shorter fasting times and also the reduction in the number of Holy Days of Obligation. On the other hand one could claim that life for Catholics has become harder because of the great store which the Council set by conscience. If the 'People of God' are meant to develop an informed conscience and a more mature*

understanding of their faith then the demands are in fact much greater. Would you agree?

This is a very interesting question. A lot of people forget that some of the things that have really rather altered the whole of our way of life, in some ways, are pre-conciliar. They go back to Pope Pius XII. One of the most dramatic things was the abolition or the quasi-abolition of the Eucharistic fast. Originally one could never go to Holy Communion or say Mass unless one fasted from midnight. One couldn't even have a drink of water from Midnight of the previous day. It was a very great imposition for some priests and people to have to remain fasting for a twelve o'clock or one o'clock Mass. You couldn't ever have Mass in the afternoons or evenings. Now the alteration of that one thing has had a most tremendous effect on what a lot of people would call the 'break-up' of the old tradition. It affected the whole question of evening devotions because evening Masses became possible. Admittedly it had been initiated gradually. The first thing was that you could have a glass of water. The second thing was that there should be just a three hour fast and then eventually it came to the one hour fast (in the time of Paul VI). It was a mitigation of what was or could be a very, very difficult act of discipline. Now, people forget that this relaxation happened before Vatican II.

I think you're right when you say that in some ways it has become harder to practise one's Faith than it was before because of the launching on to every individual's conscience of total responsibility; and not only that, but making them realise that their conscience is something that needs to be educated, to be formed. This is something that still is not happening in the ways that it should. There are many misinformed consciences to-day. The ordinary person when he hears about freedom of conscience thinks it means you can do whatever you like and that it will be all right. Well in a sense we've got to credit people with good faith even in that and never make rash judgments. But there hasn't been adequate leadership and so I would think that you are right when you say that if you are really taking seriously trying to become a committed Christian, a committed Catholic, it can be harder than it used to be. On the other hand you have got to remember also that the Church has always prided herself that she is a Church of sinners as well as saints. We are all sinners really, but the Church has always prided herself that people clung to the Faith even when sin had impaired their practice. So somehow or other you have to synthesise these two aspects of the Faith. You have a good example of it in the scriptures with the penitent thief and the way he turned to God at the last moment. We cannot change human nature and so we have got to bear in mind the great charity that is called for by Christ Himself.

> *One cannot talk about the Catholic Church in the 1960s without mentioning the encyclical 'Humanae Vitae': the Pope's decision about the Church's teaching on birth control given in 1968. Was that decision the one which you expected Paul VI to reach?*

Yes. I never thought it could possibly be otherwise because the most authentic and explicit condemnation of birth prevention was given by Pope Pius XI many years previously in the encyclical *Casti Connubi*. This document made absolutely explicit and crystallised the age-long teaching of the Church. Marriage is a Sacrament and the whole notion of the relationship between a man and a woman in marriage is that it should always be open to the begetting of a family. And so when Pope Paul VI appointed a Commission to consider this question and to advise him about it, I found it very puzzling that anyone could think for a moment that the situation could be changed. Ultimately it was entirely a matter for the solemn magisterium of the Church which Pope Paul VI unhesitatingly proclaimed; and I would say that the world-wide episcopate was entirely behind him.

> *We have just been discussing the issue of conscience, the importance attached to conscience in the post conciliar period. There are many Catholic married couples who believe in all conscience that to be good parents, to raise their children, to educate them and to do their best for them in every way, they need to be able to regulate the size of their family. What in a pastoral way can one say to people like that given the Church's teaching?*

Well I'm glad you ask 'in a pastoral way' because that is the way that I would want always to interpret *Humanae Vitae*. People have just hit on this one thing out of *Humanae Vitae* which taken as a whole is a very beautiful and a holy explanation of the sacrament of matrimony and the responsibility of parenthood and so it ought to be read in its full context. It is one of the most important documents of the century and combines guidance with deep compassion. Moreover, there is no contradiction between this document and the promotion of responsible parenthood: and indeed its calling for a greater exploration of legitimate means to enable this has resulted in entirely new knowledge, which has already offered solutions far less harmful than the prescribed practices.

In addition, *Humanae Vitae* urged the greatest gentleness and compassion, especially in the confessional. A confessor should always encourage people who are finding things difficult to be true to their Faith but never to feel that they have got to drift away from God's church. In other words, it is important that they should continue to go to Mass and continue to frequent the Sacrament of Confession to confess any departure from the Church's teaching. The matter of conscience is not always understood by people as clearly as it should be. The conscience, to be a true conscience, has got to be truly informed. A Catholic, and any Christian to my mind, is bound to inform his own conscience according to the teachings of Christ. But of course, not everyone is capable of doing that: and so there are some people who will resort to contraception thinking that their conscience is clear. If they really have been incapable of forming their conscience more clearly they can have acted justifiably because God has given the gift of conscience. But He does expect people always to be ready to try to inform their own consciences more fully with the clear teachings of Christianity.

In the confessional one has tried always to give great encouragement to people and to be very tolerant of lapses because unfortunately that's part of our fallen human nature. This calls for kindness and gentleness. It's very easy for people to get matters of sex out of proportion and forget all the other commandments. Indeed one needs to examine ones failings against the entire Decalogue. It is not easy when the media exploit sex to such a degree as to destroy the beauty of one of God's greatest gifts. I have great sympathy with young people today because they have a much harder time to get through adolescence than we had when we were young. The departure from Christian principles in this regard has conned and trapped them and all too often reduced them to a degradation from which it is not easy to emerge. They need all our compassion and help. I have absolutely no doubt at all that the clear teaching of the

Church is something very important in this matter and always will be and there is no way of avoiding this fact despite the unhelpful comment we sometimes get, even from our own press. Nevertheless, sooner or later, God's Church will be seen to be true to the promises of Christ in the guidance which she gives.

> *The year before the encyclical on birth control, in 1967, parliament passed the Abortion Act. This is probably the clearest example of an issue which is at one and the same time both moral and political. There have been a number of others since, given developments in medical science and science generally. How do you feel the Church should try to influence political issues or the political process: do you feel for example that it is best for Bishops to go public on these kinds of things or is it more effective for them to try and exert influence behind the scenes?*

I think that Abortion and the appalling increase of abortions is one of the most terrifying things that has happened in the twentieth century. To me it could easily call down the vengeance of Heaven. It is something for which this country deserves to be punished and in a sense we are all responsible for that. We haven't played the part that we should have done in seeing that this sort of anti-Christian teaching is never made legal. Altogether it is a very frightening escalation of a pagan view of life. The most important thing of all in this regard was highlighted by the Archbishop of Liverpool recently when he said that there are far too few of our people who are going into public life. There should be far more of our people going into the Trade Unions. There should be far more of our people going into politics. This is the best way that the Christian ethos and especially the Catholic ethos can be put across.

> *So being in the political arena is not simply a question for bishops, it is a question for Catholics and Christians generally?*

Above all it is for the whole people of God and this is where the role of the laity comes in. Our people should be urged to proclaim their Faith in all spheres of Government and Society. Having Catholic bishops in the House of Lords is not the answer. We Catholic bishops have always felt that our strength lies in our being 'non-establishment'. The Parliamentary field whether in Lords or Commons is for our laity. It is for the Catholic peers to use their influence in the House of Lords and for the Catholic members of parliament to do the same in the House of Commons. And we should be urging our people to enter more fully into the life of the nation. That is their role and recently Pope John Paul II in his Apostolic Exhortations on the Laity has said precisely that.

It is up to the priest more than the Bishop to encourage the people of his parish to enter into politics and in order to do so he has got to make them realise what the main principles are. Many of them nowadays don't need to have this said to them but he should be there to encourage them and to inspire them rather than interfering himself directly. That would be my view.

This whole question brings to mind the Justice and Peace Commission of the Leeds Diocese, which was established soon after I became Bishop. This development attracted a considerable amount of interest in other parts of the country as something emerging specifically from Vatican II. It was important that such a commission should have an expertise which would give it balance in terms of its approach to what are often highly politicised questions. This was imparted to it by Anne Forbes, who became a national and indeed international figure in this respect. We owe her a great debt of gratitude, as well as others like John Battle M.P., who gave a great lead to our laity in playing a responsible role in the life of the country. In this context the Church was splendidly served also by Stanley Cohen, especially when he served in Parliament. The same phenomenon, of course, happened in the local areas and in this regard I must mention the devoted contribution of John Power in Leeds and Dr Brian Quinn in Halifax. John Power served as a magistrate with great distinction for many years especially in his capacity as Chairman of the Juvenile Bench; now he is one of Her Majesty's Deputy-Lord Lieutenants for West Yorkshire. Dr Quinn has been a leading member of the medical profession in Halifax and was instrumental in establishing the town's centre for the care of the terminally ill. Both of them have also given a great lead at different times to our own Diocesan Pastoral Council. So, lay people are active in many spheres but the need is for many more to follow the example of men and women like these.

> *You mentioned Archbishop Worlock of Liverpool, who has adopted a very public posture in recent years defending and promoting the interests, as he sees them, of the people of Liverpool in a period of high unemployment and great social problems in that city. He has found his admirers for that, but he has also found his detractors who see him taking a kind of party political stance in opposition to the policies of a particular government. Is that a danger and something which really should be avoided or is it an inevitable part of being a witness to the Gospel?*

I would say it is an interim responsibility in a time when the people have not fully entered into the political arena themselves both locally and nationally. Somebody else has got to be holding the fort in the meantime. You need the Christian voice and if the Christian Voice is not coming articulately from the people in the way that it should - and please God it will - as an interim thing this *Vox Ecclesiae* has got to be heard. Archbishop Worlock has been outstanding in the great ecumenical lead that he has given in union with the Anglican Bishop of Liverpool, David Shepherd. And together they have proclaimed the social teaching of the Church very much as manifested in the great Papal Encyclicals.

> *When you became Bishop of Leeds in 1966 how did you set about implementing your policies in the light of Vatican II. You have already told us of your belief in dialogue and delegation as Administrator of Westminster Cathedral. Was this also a guiding principle for you as a diocesan bishop?*

Yes. I believe that one's providential placements in life all contribute to the ultimate things that one is asked to do, such as being the Bishop of a large Diocese. Therefore I look back to all the experience that I had by virtue of my earlier placements, and the people that I met who had a great influence on my life. I have often spoken of Monsignor Duchemin, the Rector of the Beda. He had a famous saying: "Never be content with the second best; try always to go for the first best." Having always tried to do that when I was Administrator at Westminster Cathedral I learnt a different lesson when I became coadjutor of Middlesbrough. And it was this: that the relationship of a loving friendliness between a Bishop and his priests, and between priests and one another, is much more important than administrative efficiency. However, by God's grace the two approaches can be parallel. I always tried to be efficient. For example, I always tried to clear my desk each day and to answer letters and pay bills, especially those of the small shop-keepers, by return of post. This was often against the advice of my financial advisers who always thought that it was better to delay for a period to gain further interest on what was in hand. But I still liked to get everything cleared in that sort of way very quickly. I don't think that this was pride. I think there can be a sort of justice in the fact, that one is concerned about people sometimes getting into real trouble because cheques haven't been sent out at the right time.

I also think that it is very important to delegate and when I was the Administrator at Westminster Cathedral I had a large staff. This made it necessary to place trust in each individual and to delegate in a big way. If anyone asked me which of the appointments in my life I would have chosen myself, I think there is only one I would have selected. I have found great happiness in all of them for there is a great satisfaction in knowing that you are in this or that assignment by the Church's choice and backing. So, my style of management, if you would like to put it in those sort of terms, was a style that emerged from the experiences I myself had had, the backing I had had, the inspiration that I had from other people, and the guidance that I had had from them. Before I became a Bishop I learnt a great deal from the way Cardinal Hinsley and Cardinal Griffin supported me in my work in London. I think that all one's life one has to look for guidance, not only from God in time of prayer, but also from those who are one's superiors, and those who are one's collaborators at every level. I hope I always had a happy relationship with my fellow priests and later with my fellow Bishops despite my mistakes and failings.

> *As a believer in delegation and collaboration are there particular individuals to whom you turned for assistance during your time as Bishop of Leeds?*

Very much so; especially my Vicars General. I inherited a wonderful Vicar General in Monsignor John Joseph Kelly, a lovely character from County Tyrone who was always affectionately known as 'J.J.'. In the interregnum following Bishop Dwyer's appointment to Birmingham he had been the Vicar Capitular of the Diocese and many people thought he would become the new Bishop. When I became Bishop he backed me absolutely from the beginning and was a great source of help to me in getting to know people and especially with regard to making clerical appointments. He was a very wise old chap - I say old but he wasn't much older than me - and for many years he was a tower of strength to me. It was a great sadness when he fell victim to a stroke in 1971 which ultimately made it impossible for him to carry on with administrative duties. Nevertheless, he remained a Vicar General until his death in 1980 and also a very close friend whom I used to consult about many issues. In 1968 the Holy See appointed an Auxiliary Bishop to the Diocese of Leeds who became, at the same time, also a Vicar General. This was Monsignor Gerald Moverley, hitherto the Chancellor of the Diocese. In 1971 he was joined by Monsignor Kevin O'Brien. He was a priest of the Leeds Diocese who had been Superior of the Catholic Missionary Society for the previous 11 years. Following Monsignor Kelly's stroke he agreed to return to the Diocese and become Vicar General. He was very highly thought of throughout the country and had wide experience of all the different dioceses of the country through giving missions and retreats.

When I came to the Diocese of Leeds I had very useful conversations with two former Bishops of Leeds: one was Cardinal Heenan and the other was Archbishop Dwyer. I consulted them, for example, on what had seemed to me to be a very obvious necessity, especially in the light of Vatican II: the division of the Diocese. The Sheffield area seemed to me of an entirely different character from the northern parts of the Diocese, and it did seem that there was something to be said for a subdivision of this great Diocese of Leeds. The first time I went to Sheffield it was made very clear to me that they didn't look north to Leeds but southwards. All that quadrilateral of Doncaster, Barnsley, Rotherham and Sheffield was a very different world from Huddersfield, Halifax, Wakefield, Leeds, Bradford, York, Ripon and so forth.

Soon after I came to Leeds I attended a function in Sheffield at which the Master Cutler told me that the southern area ought to be a separate Diocese, and that the beautiful church of St Marie would make a very fine cathedral. I came more and more to his opinion, in consultation with others and indeed in consultation with my predecessors. This prospect was also encouraged by the 'Ground Plan' produced for the achievement of greater pastoral efficiency in the light of the decrees of the Council.

When you were provided with an Auxiliary Bishop for the Leeds Diocese he effectively became an area Bishop for South Yorkshire?

This was Bishop Moverley who was appointed in 1968 to whom I owe more than I can ever repay. He effectively became area Bishop because I gave him every possible jurisdiction in the Sheffield area. It soon became very clear to me that I should ask Rome to initiate procedures regarding a new diocese. In this I had the co-operation of the Bishop of Nottingham. It was a long process but eventually it happened and Bishop Moverley became the first Bishop of Hallam in 1980. He has done splendid work despite considerable ill health. But it was that mark of the Cross that seemed to assist greatly in the development of the new Diocese of Hallam. This was all very much in accord with the decrees of the Council. As I understood them they called for smaller dioceses rather than for area Bishops.

With the creation of the Hallam Diocese you lost an Auxiliary who had also acted as Vicar General, so you were left with the one Vicar General for the Diocese of Leeds. Did you then appoint a second Vicar General?

No. There was no need to at that stage but when Bishop O'Brien was made an Auxiliary Bishop of Middlesbrough in 1981, I felt that I did need two Vicars General. I wanted to have one who was Yorkshire bred as well as one who was Irish because of the great number of Irish priests in the Diocese. Accordingly I appointed Monsignor John Murphy, who came originally from County Cork, and had been the Administrator of the Diocesan Catholic Child Welfare Society, together with Monsignor Peter McGuire who was a Selby man and Administrator of St Anne's Cathedral. The two of them served me with great dedication, and loyalty. With them as my assistants I continued my policy to delegate but never to abdicate!

When you arrived in Leeds in 1966 you not only inherited an administrative set-up but also a domestic one, including a chauffeur who has become part of diocesan folklore.

Charles Walker was the chauffeur whom I inherited from my predecessors when I became Bishop of Leeds. In fact he had been employed in this capacity by the Diocese since Bishop Cowgill's time. When we moved to Eltofts, in the autumn in 1966, he came to live in a cottage there on the campus and was a very faithful and devoted chauffeur. I think all the Bishops for whom he worked regarded him as a considerable character and there were some very amusing stories about him. Two are connected with Bishop Heenan. The first is about the time he thought he was due for a wage rise and he said to the Bishop's Chaplain: "Do you think now is a good time for me to ask the Bishop to put up my wages?" The Chaplain replied "No don't do it at the moment, Walker. You see, Lent has just started and he's given up his pipe. I should leave it till later on if I were you." So Walker left it until Eastertide and he told me that he was driving Bishop Heenan around in the car one day and they were waiting for somebody else to join them. At that moment Walker thought it would be a good opportunity to ask the Bishop to raise his wages. He was just about to do so when a newspaper boy passed the car shouting out "Bishop of Leeds appointed Archbishop of Liverpool." So that kiboshed that one. Bishop Heenan, however, was there for some time before he went on to Liverpool. "So," said Walker "I was driving him along the Ring Road and he was in the back of the car, and I thought I would have another go at it and as I drove along I said to him "Don't you think, My Lord, it is time that my wages were put up?" A voice from the back said "It is no use asking me, Walker. You see, I am no longer Bishop of Leeds, I am the Archbishop Elect of Liverpool." Walker said "I felt right mad. When we came to the next lay-by I pulled in and I switched off the engine and turned round to him and said "Look here, I am supposed to be chauffeur to the Bishop of Leeds, if you're the Archbishop Elect of Liverpool what are you doing in this car?" However, I think he must have said something to his successor, because the first thing Bishop Dwyer did on his arrival in Leeds was to put up my wages."

The following story is about the time he took me to Weetwood in Leeds to see the house that Bishop Poskitt had bought and lived in. It was a very lovely place and as we drove away I said to Walker "Why do you think that Bishop Heenan left Weetwood?" There was silence for a moment or two, which surprised me. Then he said "Do you mind if I stick my neck out?" and I said "No." He said "Well he was like a hen that wanted to lay an egg and didn't know where to lay it." I remember passing this story on to some of my confreres in the hierarchy later on; they thought it was a very apt description in some respects of Doctor Heenan!

Charles Walker eventually retired, after his wife died, and went to live with his daughter in Aylesbury. He used to come back to Eltofts and we always gave him a great welcome. When he died we had his funeral in St. Edward's Church, Clifford where he is buried beside his wife. Never again did we mange to afford another chauffeur.

As a Bishop for more than twenty years you were part of the collective leadership of the Catholic Church in England and Wales. In 1964 when you began your episcopate was there such an institution as the Bishops' Conference?

Yes there was and it is important to realise this. There has always been a gathering once or twice a year of all the Ordinaries of the country. I say the Ordinaries because until recent times Auxiliary Bishops were not included. In Archbishop's House, Westminster, you will find that the upper library has a horseshoe table round which the bishops sat with the Cardinal of Westminster at the head. But the horseshoe table has now fallen out of use because the number of bishops has greatly increased, especially with the appointment of additional Auxiliaries. There are now over forty bishops and so it is necessary to have a much larger space in which to meet. But the gatherings did exist and it is important to realise that, because a lot of people think that the Conference is something entirely new. The gathering was given a new impetus by the Council in the sense that when we were in Rome we were constantly meeting together to discuss the impact of the different decrees on the life of the Church in our country. This has continued and now it is *de rigeur* that each bishop is part of the Conference of Bishops. You are expected, as a Bishop, to go to the meetings each year, in Low Week and in the autumn, and at various other times.

Until Archbishop Heenan was appointed to Westminster, it had been the custom that the Archbishop of Westminster was *ipso facto* the Chairman of the Hierarchy Conference. Heenan got that changed. Having been a Bishop in the time when it was not the custom for Catholic Bishops to retire (as they now normally do at the age of 75) he thought that it was important that we should elect a new Chairman every five years. A new constitution was inaugurated and the Holy See cancelled the ruling that the Archbishop of Westminster should be the *praeses perpetuus* of the conference. That is why for part of the time I was a member of the conference, Archbishop Dwyer was the Chairman. Archbishop Hume was made *praeses* some time after he became a Cardinal, after a year or so at Westminster, and so far he has always been reelected.

> *We have mentioned the sixties and the aftermath of the Council and how at the centre of the Church Paul VI had to contend with all the problems of that period. Of course, in England and Wales it was very much Cardinal Heenan who was confronted with this challenge. Looking back now would you say he coped with the situation effectively?*

I think he became remarkably open-minded. I think he pushed us too far ahead very quickly over the devolution, so to speak, of the liturgy. The transfer to the vernacular called for very much more preparation. I would like to have seen it done much more gently. It engendered a lot of opposition which might have been obviated had it been better prepared. But, it is easy to be wise after the event.

> *Initially many people must have thought Basil Hume to be an unusual choice as Heenan's successor. A man who had spent most of his life in a monastic environment and had spent the whole of the post Vatican II period at Ampleforth as Abbot of the community. Yet he became, in the middle of the 1970s, the leader of the Church in England and Wales. What lay behind this appointment?*

I imagine that, humanly speaking, it came about because for one reason or another there was no very obvious candidate of the right age in the existing hierarchy. There was also a feeling in some quarters that we needed a new image. Given these two lines of thinking the Abbot of Ampleforth was a fairly obvious candidate. His strong spiritual background and gift of leadership were alike well-known and combined with a typical English understatement have surely produced an inspired appointment. The new image which was sought has certainly come about and the Archbishop of Westminster has become in a sense even more of a national figure than Cardinal Manning in the 19th Century and Cardinal Hinsley in the period of the Second World War.

Given the debate about 'collegiality' in the government of the Universal Church since Vatican II how do you see the role of the national episcopal conferences in relation to the authority of the Papacy?

The debate about the exact role of the Bishops' Conference still continues, though the picture in general is fairly clear. One has got to remember that Vatican I finished because of the Franco-Prussian War. If it had gone on it would certainly have said something more about the relationship of the Bishops of the world with the successor of St Peter but it didn't have the time or a chance to do that. In one sense Vatican II has completed Vatican I. That is why I am always saying it is so important, historically, to see Vatican II in the context of everything that has gone before it. It is particularly so in this matter, because it was made absolutely clear that the validity of all that Vatican I did forever stands.. What it didn't have time to do was to relate fully the universal local episcopate to the infallibility of the Pope. First of all it is surely clear that the Church must be infallible if it is going to do what Our Lord has promised that it should do. How does the infallibility of the Church work? It works with the successor of St Peter and with all the Bishops of the world and they are not disunited, they speak as one voice. Now in addition to the successor of St Peter there is a special autonomy (but not an infallibility) that has been given in the Church since its earliest days to the local Bishop. Accordingly one has to understand that there is a very special role for the successor of St Peter, and indeed for all the Bishops of the world gathered together with him. There is also a very special role for an individual Bishop of a Diocese in his relationship with the Holy See and with his fellow bishops throughout the world.

Now, when you ask me about the Bishops' Conferences, I would say that I cannot envisage they will ever be regarded in their independent units as a magisterium because everything has to be done in the Church universally and it is not just one country or one body of people who can make a magisterial decision. The same thing applies to a Synod. There is no comparison in either to what happens in a gathering of the Universal Church in union with the Apostolic See. Therefore, it is a very interesting question that is on the table, nowadays, as to the exact authority of a 'Conference' of Bishops. One can understand this in our country because we always had a 'Conference' long before Vatican II in that all the bishops of the country met once or twice a year to discuss common problems. It seems to me that this "Conference' idea is fundamentally and rightly a continuation of that. It hasn't happened like that in all parts of the world but now generally speaking it is taking place. But there remain, for example, individual local bishops who do not belong to a 'Conference' officially. It would be foolish if an individual Ordinary didn't go because of the enrichment that it can be to his own experience and the contribution that he could make to the total picture. Therefore, I would say that it would be quite impossible to think of the American Conference of Bishops or any other national or international conference of bishops as being total in any sense in itself. It is only valid to my mind in the great power and authority of the local bishop together with the great power and final authority of the successor of St Peter, which always reflects the Universal Church. Nowadays the Holy Father frequently consults all the bishops of the world about anything that is of great consequence. Despite the under-development of communications in the past, there was always as close a relationship as could be in the circumstances.

We seem to be coming back to the point that for you the Papacy is an institution of supreme importance.

Indeed, otherwise why would Our Lord have done what he did in the Gospels and why would the whole history of the Church from the earliest times have been centred on this? It goes back to the Scriptures and the earliest eras of the Church's life. This isn't just a Catholic conception. It is also the understanding of a number of Anglicans. The late Professor Jalland of Exeter, whom I knew quite well, wrote a very fine book on **Ubi Petrus, ibi Ecclesia** - 'Where Peter is, there is the Church' and you get this in St Augustine and all the way through history. I used to know an Anglican Canon, called de Satge, who wrote an extremely good book on the primacy and not only the primacy but the infallibility of the successor of St Peter: because Our Lord promised him, "your faith will not fail". It seems to me absolutely unthinkable that one can leave Peter and, therefore, his successors also, out of the picture. The sad thing is the drifting away of the oriental Church in the 11th century. But this was very largely because they had a very deep and keen sense of the autonomy of the local Ordinary and this remains an important element in the Church's life. Please God they will come to see that you can't preach the Gospel of Christ, without the primacy and infallibility that he gave to Peter. That is my own commitment and I would die for it.

More than any of his predecessors, of course, Pope John Paul II has in practical ways demonstrated the universality of the Catholic Church by his travels. Are you a supporter of these activities? Is it a good use of the Pope's time and resources?

There is everything to be said for what Pope John Paul II is doing because he is carrying out the commission of Christ; "confirm your brethren". We need him to strengthen his brother bishops throughout the world and his travels enable him to do this in a very personal way. God give him the strength to continue and his successors to do the same. The personal contact has a very considerable impact.

It has some disadvantages from the point of view of the central administration of the Church in Rome. The new technology of instantaneous contact with the Pope wherever he may be may well help that situation however. And I would think that gradually a new picture is likely to emerge, due to technological development, which will allow an ever closer relationship between Curia and individual Bishops. Most, I think, would tell you even now that far from being inhibited by what is known as the 'Roman Curia', which unfortunately has a low rating in the press and the mass media, its members are a great source of strength to us and highly efficient and very anxious to serve the whole Church. As long as that note of service is always kept, the situation will always be satisfactory. I do remember one friend of mine saying to me "I much preferred it when Popes were the prisoners of the Vatican" because that meant that everything was attended to by return of post from Rome. It isn't always so easy now but that is something which is in the process of being solved.

You have described the episcopate's relationship with the Roman Curia as being somewhat different from the public image. Have the representatives of the Holy See in this country always been of help and support to bishops in England and Wales or did you feel that perhaps they had a kind of 'policeman' like role?

No I never felt that: though one did have one or two trivial experiences of that kind, earlier on, but never in later years. In the Council itself there was a feeling that the representatives of the Holy See could easily be laymen, but that doesn't seem to have come about. Today, representatives of the Holy See in different countries are trying to reflect something of the international thinking of the Holy Father, and also to show the warm pastoral aspect of their assignment. Our present Pro-nuncio, for example, is going round the different dioceses quite extensively and evidently it is the mind of Rome that he should try to bring new strength and new courage to the local churches from the See of Peter. There are different views about these things, but I can only say that I have had nothing but kindness and great help, all my priestly and episcopal life, from the Apostolic Nunciature.

As Bishop of Leeds you travelled to Rome on several occasions to make an 'Ad Limina' visit to the Holy See. What purpose do such visits serve and what did you derive from them?

I have stressed already the great importance of a Bishop's relationship with the Successor of St Peter. From time to time he needs wise guidance and always he needs the assurance that he is following the right paths. It is because of this that there has grown up over the centuries the custom of regular visits by diocesan Bishops to the Holy See. In part, these are always a kind of pilgrimage. The very term *Ad Limina* refers to an episcopal visit to the threshold of the Apostles. The Bishop is bidden pray at the Tombs of SS Peter and Paul. He is also called to greet and confer with the reigning Pope, Successor of the Apostle Peter. In addition he usually calls at some, if not all, the central offices of the different departments of the Universal Church. This can be a very enriching experience; for he can often call on the enlightenment of great expertise regarding many different problems. These visits are usually quinquennial. But they may also happen more often. I have always found them a source of encouragement and assurance. It is very unfair that the Roman Curia often gets a bad press. We know that all bureaucracy has its dangers. But in our times there is a great realisation amongst those who man these universal entities that they are there to serve. And generally speaking I can only say that I have had good service and great understanding. I always came home refreshed and encouraged.

What impression of Pope John Paul II have you taken away from your meetings with him?

Cardinal Wiseman once wrote a book on his recollections of four Popes in the middle years of the 19th century. It is extremely entertaining as well as historically enriching. Any one of us today could, I am sure, give fascinating reminiscences of the Popes of the 20th century. I have described elsewhere my first audience with Pope Pius XI in 1936, and I could write a chapter on each of his successors apart from John Paul I who only served for 30 days. For I had a number of Audiences as a Priest with Pius XII and John XXIII. And even more as a Bishop with Paul VI and John Paul II.

They were all memorable occasions in their different ways. The most intimate and deeply spiritual ones were with Pope Paul VI. But each of the others had their own charisma. They all conveyed something quite special. The motto of Pius XI was *Fides Intrepida* and he radiated intrepid Faith. Pius XII seemed to combine and exhale the wisdom of the ages. And John XXIII, with the word "coraggio" always on his lips imparted a dynamic empowering of God's fidelity to those whom He had called to His special service. Paul VI was quite different: I think, in a sense, he was a great listener and deeply *simpatico*.

John Paul II brought a new dimension to his brother bishops on their *Ad Limina* visits with many frequent concelebrations, and working breakfasts, lunches and suppers. The energy of the man, as all the world knows, is beyond all understanding. And the love and the caring which he radiates has made him entirely unique. Some put it down to his Slav origins; others to the vicissitudes through which he has passed. There is no doubt that here is a great Man of God.

Providence has always produced potentially the right man for the current years. If some others have not used their potentialities in the best way, there is no doubt about John Paul II. His correspondence with his gifts must be as unique as the plethora of the gifts themselves.

> *In 1982, of course, the Holy Father came to Great Britain, in a sense one of the most historic events to have taken place during recent years. It took place against an unfortunate background: the outbreak of the Falklands War just a few weeks before he was due to arrive. That threw the whole visit into some doubt until almost the very last minute. Presumably you were intimately involved in the preparations and indeed the negotiations which were required because of the Falklands situation. Were you always confident that the visit would be made as planned?*

By no means. We understood completely once the Falkland War had started that it might be impossible for the Holy Father to come because he had always been very careful never to take sides in differences between countries. It was clear that the Pope saw his visit to our country first and foremost as a pastoral event. Fortunately the discussions which took place during April and May 1982 resulted in his decision to come here on precisely those terms. It was obviously a great relief to hear of that decision especially when one considers the great preparations which had been made for his visit.

> *Would you say that the Papal Visit of 1982 was a successful one for the Catholic Church in this country?*

Without question, I have no reservations about that at all. Of course, it wasn't possible to attend all the events but we were all down in Westminster for his arrival and that afternoon after the great Mass in Westminster Cathedral, he went to Southwark Cathedral. A number of us went with him there. I couldn't go to Canterbury because I had to come back to Leeds in order to get ready for the northern events, and to go on to Liverpool to greet him with the other Northern Bishops when he came there. I am very glad to say that I saw both the Canterbury and other events, which I missed, very fully on television but I would have loved to have been present at all of them and especially, as a former Westminster priest, at the Wembley Mass.

We met the Holy Father at Speke Airport and took part in the great drive through Liverpool, calling in at the Anglican Cathedral, and culminating in the Mass at the Metropolitan Cathedral. The day ended with dinner with the Holy Father at Archbishop's House in Liverpool, where he stayed the night. I then had to drive to Hazlewood Castle so as to get to York in time to say the Mass at 7.30 am for the assembling crowds. The Holy Father was due to arrive by helicopter in the early afternoon after a morning Mass in Heaton Park Manchester. The York event was especially connected with us. The original co-ordinator for this was Fr Francis Gresham OP, a native of Bradford and a priest of the Leeds Diocese until he joined the Dominicans in the early 1960s. He became chaplain to York University and was appointed to oversee the preparations for the Pope's visit to York. Sadly he died very suddenly early in 1982 and I then lent my own secretary, Father Arthur Roche, to organise the whole affair, which he did very admirably. It was a glorious day and the theme of the Pope's homily was family life. It was indeed a very moving occasion. He went on again in a helicopter from us to RAF Leeming and then to Scotland. After the Scottish visit he came down to Cardiff. I travelled down to Cardiff and concelebrated with him in the Pontcanna fields. I was in the Castle in Cardiff when he received the Freedom of the City and then we drove on to the great gathering of youth, which was one of the most moving events of the whole visit. Finally we all went with him in a vast cavalcade to Cardiff airport from where he flew back to Rome.

These were great events as most people would agree. But do you think the Pope's visit has had any longer lasting effects?

It is very difficult to assess that. However, a lot of things registered over a long period. A booklet was printed of all the speeches that the Holy Father made. Most of us bishops quoted them at various times. For example, at York the Pope gave a beautiful discourse on family life: there were others on youth and many other topics. That booklet became quite a text book of meditation for us and I still use it quite a lot: reminding people of what he said on various occasions. I am sure that the visit must have had an impact. It meant above all that the Catholic Church had really come to a certain maturity in this country.

The Pope's visit reminded us very clearly that we are part of the Universal Church. In a particular way the Leeds Diocese has long been aware of that fact through its mission in Peru. Perhaps you could explain how that came about and its purpose?

It came about before my time as Bishop of Leeds because it had been started by Archbishop Dwyer when he was Bishop of Leeds. It was one result of the growing sense of universal responsibility, especially with regard to people in the Third World. My predecessor had, therefore, very wisely inquired as to how best he could help in the shanty towns of Lima, the capital of Peru. Already there were tens of thousands of people coming down from the mountain regions to the coastal cities for employment, and education; a lot of them were destitute. Bishop Dwyer got in touch with the Columban Fathers in Ireland, who already had a very large mission in Peru, and asked how he could best contribute. They suggested that he send out two or three priests, which he did and, therefore, I inherited that commitment. It had been put to the Diocese that this was a very important undertaking both spiritually and materially. And so, there were very considerable collections in different parts of the Diocese for the Peru Mission.

In 1968, I went to Peru myself to see the priests working there and to weigh up the situation. I was accompanied by Father Tony Wilkinson who had been in Peru himself. He had come back to the Diocese after a stay of five years in Peru which was the norm for most of our priests. We flew to New York and then down to Jamaica where we stayed for a little break of twenty-four hours at Montego Bay. We then flew on right across South America to Lima where on our arrival at the airport we were greeted in the early hours of the morning by all the priests and sisters in the area. This they seem to do if anybody is going out from this part of the world. It was certainly a VIP welcome. I was escorted then into the main house of the Columban Fathers which was on the outskirts of the old Spanish city, very near to the Barriada where the shanty towns are situated.

I stayed to begin with in a bungalow in the grounds of the Columban Fathers' headquarters. The first night I was there I was woken up by earth tremors. When I awoke I thought, having been in London houses and churches built over the underground railway, that Lima must have an underground also and turned over and went to sleep again. I found later that morning that all the people with any sense had come out into the open because that could have been the prelude to an earthquake. It didn't happen, I'm glad to say on that occasion. From there I went to all the different parishes of the Barriada. One had been run by Father Burke, now in the Diocese of Hallam. I stayed in his presbytery there and experienced first hand some of the difficulties of a priest's life in Peru. For example, there was no water laid on and buckets of water were brought in from a tanker. The floor of the house was plain earth. Despite such hardships the people were wonderful, full of joy and very lovable, especially the children. They were devoted to the priests, with whom they had a very close relationship. The Masses were mostly held in the open-air and usually started long after the supposed time. The heat was very intense at the time I was there. There hadn't been any rain for decades and, therefore, all the hills round about were covered with a deep brown dust. Because of the lack of irrigation there was no greenery anywhere and the landscape was a somewhat depressing sight. This was redeemed however by a beautiful blue sky and glorious sunshine. The Pacific Ocean in the far distance and the mountains enhanced what was otherwise a very poor area.

I visited some of the adobe houses which were all one storey dwellings. In the main room you would have the hens and the guinea pigs running round. Occasionally there was a pig if the inhabitants were rich! I can remember going to one house and they asked me if I could stay to lunch: if so they would wish me to tell them which of the guinea pigs running around the room I would like them to slaughter. Fortunately, I had another engagement!

I went round the other Barriada with the Columban Fathers and the sisters. The sisters, who had come from Ireland and elsewhere to help the Fathers, played a great part in many of the parishes. The people turned to them in a special way because they could give them great help educationally, medically, and in innumerable other ways. In Peru they had never known nuns other than enclosed nuns and so when they found various Orders working in parishes it was something very new to them. It created a very great apostolate for those nuns both in teaching and in nursing and in looking after them in all sorts of ways. So one of the main things that I did when I came back to England was to try to persuade some nuns to go out there to assist our priests. That made a very big difference because I had a lovely response from the Sisters of Mercy, in particular, and later from the Franciscans as well. They came to play and still are playing a tremendous part in our contribution to the life of the Barriada in Peru.

Of course, while I was there I travelled around and I saw the old Spanish city of Lima itself and its beautiful shrines of St Rose and St Martin de Porres. Then I went up to the great Inca civilisation centre, Cuzco. That was quite an experience because the altitude is very great and when you land from the plane you reel and stagger like a drunken man. They tell you that you must, when you arrive at the hotel, go and lie down for an hour or two before you think of walking anywhere. At the time I went there, there was a strike on. One sympathised greatly with the strikers because they were all employed by the government and the government hadn't paid any of their salaries for many months. The only way they could galvanise things into action was to strike. The area was full of troops of the Peruvian Army. It was quite an alarming experience being taken about in army trucks. I was very glad when I got back to Lima, despite the excitement of seeing the remains of the amazing civilisation of the Incas.

I also went to Trujillo where the Bishop of Cork, Dr Lucey, had founded several parishes, each one with a church, a presbytery, a convent, a hall, a school and sometimes a hospital and each one a part of the Diocese of Cork. It was a tremendous achievement but it wasn't a pattern that everyone followed. It was however the most efficient site that I saw from the point of view of the Church's life in Peru at that time. There have been many developments since. When we came back the Diocesan Peru Commission was formed which made the whole of the West Riding conscious of the needs in Peru. Events staged in support of our Priests and Sisters multiplied and a Diocesan Collection was also imposed. People rallied round in a remarkable way for which I was deeply grateful. At times, I wondered whether it would be possible to get more lay people to go out there. But the cost of travel is so great and then there is the question of the language. I became aware that more could be done effectively by paying for the services of a Peruvian person than to send people out. From the point of view of the local people that has great possibilities.

> *If we may, perhaps we could return from South America to more familiar territory. By birth you are a Yorkshireman, although you were educated in Lancashire and later in Oxford, and have spent much of your life in the south of England. In 1964 you returned to Yorkshire, and I wonder what it meant to you to return to the North and to Yorkshire in particular?*

You might say that I took to it again like a duck to water, and I think there are many reasons for that besides the fact that I was Yorkshire born One of them was certainly my interest in history and in ancient monuments and ancient houses. I found something very special about the ethos of Yorkshire because of the great contemplative life led here in medieval times, which in some sense still hovers here. There is a great inspiration from places like Fountains, Rievaulx, Byland, Kirkstall, and Mount Grace. Many others too radiate an atmosphere of sanctity that has never quite been lost. And, of course, you have still got the tradition kept alive in a great living monastic house like Ampleforth. It has always been a great joy to me to go to all these places and to discover something about their history.

I feel the same to some extent about the great country houses. In the Diocese of Leeds we have Carlton Towers, one of the residences of the present Duke of Norfolk, and his favourite one because he was brought up there. Then there are others like Broughton Hall, near Skipton, bearing witness to the great recusant tradition of the Tempest family, and Ripley Castle, north of Harrogate, the home of the Ingilby family. These great Catholic houses were the sort of places where people could go to hear Mass in secret and to receive all the sacraments of the Catholic Church. When we went to Rome in 1987 for the beatification of the eighty-five martyrs many of these families connected with the martyrs were represented and they took a great pride in seeing the holiness and the courage of their ancestors being highlighted by the Church. That event was very specially related to our part of the world because many of the martyrs were from hereabouts. One who is often forgotten from the Leeds viewpoint, but always remembered with very great devotion in the Middlesbrough Diocese, is Blessed Nicholas Postgate. Although he spent his latter years living on the North Yorkshire Moors, his earlier life was spent at Saxton near to Tadcaster and in the Elmet area where he was chaplain to the Catholic Lady Hungate, before he moved further north. He is, indeed, a figure who is shared with great devotion by the whole of Catholic Yorkshire, as indeed is St Margaret Clitheroe, canonised earlier.

So one finds great inspiration living in Yorkshire from all these things. I love taking people to see places like Carlton Towers, Ripley Castle and Broughton Hall where a great welcome in every case greets one and where one is carried back to the days of those who suffered so severely for their Faith.

> *In addition to the great Catholic houses you have already mentioned I think we ought to say something about the revival of Catholic life at Hazlewood Castle, for which you were largely responsible in your capacity as Bishop of Leeds.*

Soon after I had been made Bishop of Leeds, I made a visit one day to Hazlewood Castle in order to see the 14th century chapel. These lands had been given in 1067 to the Vavasour family by William the Conqueror because they had helped him to subdue Yorkshire. Although the Castle has changed a great deal since Norman times, it has a great Catholic history and the Vavasour family remained there until this century. It was no longer in their hands when I went there and it had been bought by Donald Hart who ran the Bridge Inn Restaurant on the A1 near Wetherby. He had a hobby of buying up such places and restoring them. In the case of Hazlewood, he lived there himself and was very devoted to it.

I rang the bell of the Castle and there was no answer so I went round to the back. An elderly gentleman came down the steps in dungarees and smoking a cigar and I said that I was looking for the owner of Hazlewood Castle. He said "That's me" and I told him who I was and asked him if I could see the Chapel. He said "Oh, it's not very convenient" and then he said "Anyway I'm not very pleased with the Roman Catholics." So I said "Why is that?" He said "Well, for one thing there is a Carmelite nun, in Thicket Priory in the Middlesbrough Diocese who is a member of the Vavasour family. I asked them to let her out because I wanted her to identify things that she would have known when she lived here as a girl. They wouldn't let her come out. Moreover, I try to preserve this chapel with dignity but they have moved away a very large relic which was part of the place and I don't know where it has gone." Eventually he did open the door of the chapel and showed it to me but with no great friendliness.

It occurred to me that I might do something about this situation and I got in touch with the Bishop of Middlesbrough and asked him if he would give permission for the Vavasour nun to come out for an afternoon to identify things at Hazlewood Castle. He did so, and she came to Hazlewood. It was a lovely occasion and I was there as she helped him a great deal. He was delighted and I said to her "Sister, this gentleman also tells me that there is a major relic that has been removed from this place. I don't know what it is." She said "It would be the body of a child martyr from the Roman Catacombs." So I said "How on earth did such a relic come to Hazlewood?" She said "It was given to my grandfather by Pope Pius IX for fighting against Garibaldi." So I said "Well, Mr Hart has got very good intentions. He is trying to restore and preserve this chapel. I think that relic ought to be brought back." "Well," she said "If you say so. We have got it in Thicket Priory. But that child will cry out to heaven until the Blessed Sacrament is over her head again." As indeed happened.

There was also a man staying there, a Frenchman, who was an expert in ancient carving. Mr Hart had bought some panelling from, strangely enough, a Carmelite monastery in Holland, which he fitted in to one of the rooms at Hazlewood. It was, and remains a very fine piece of work. This Frenchman told us how he had moved from one bedroom to another in the Castle because it was haunted. Whereupon the Vavasour nun said "I can assure you there was no ghost here in the Vavasour days, but I am quite prepared to believe that there is one, until it comes back into Catholic hands." Afterwards Mr Hart became very friendly and invited me to lunch in the Castle. After lunch he took me into the library where there was a log fire burning and he said "Look here, Bishop. I realise that this place ought to be in the hands of Catholics." He said "I will sell it to you cheaply if you will let me live here until I die." Well I had just bought and set up Wood Hall and I didn't feel that I could afford to do anything about it. So I said "I will have to think about it. It is very kind of you to make such a gesture." I went away wondering what I could do to bring Hazlewood back into Catholic hands again. Then I suddenly remembered that when I was in the Westminster Diocese I used to take pilgrimages down to Aylesford, where the Carmelite Fathers had turned what used to be one of their houses in medieval times into a great pilgrimage centre for the south of England and I thought "What a wonderful northern Aylesford, Hazlewood would make." So out of the blue and without knowing him, I wrote to the Provincial of the Carmelite Fathers at Aylesford and told him about the situation. To my surprise I got a letter by return of post saying "This is the most extraordinary coincidence. Your letter arrived on the morning when we were having a chapter to decide where we would make a new foundation. So I am coming up to Yorkshire now to see you". And he did, and they bought it at the price at which it had been offered to me, and they allowed Donald Hart to remain in residence. The Carmelites came to Yorkshire in 1968 and I made the parish of Tadcaster vacant for them for the time being so that they could be on the spot from the start and perhaps begin to do something with the Chapel. It was some years before Donald Hart died. When that happened the transformation began and it has become a great centre of pilgrimage and for conferences and retreats and please God it will remain so. This development was one of the greatest consolations to me in the time that I was Bishop of Leeds.

> *There are two other projects in the Leeds diocese with which you were closely involved: the development of St. Gemma's Hospice and the Clarke-Foley bequest which both show how the Church can respond to the needs of people in the modern world. How were you able to assist with those projects?*

I was involved with St Gemma's from the start, in co-operation with the Cross and Passion Nuns who have continued to maintain the hospice despite many difficulties. For many years the sisters had run a private school in North Leeds but by the mid 1970s the Order decided to withdraw from providing private schooling because the Catholic schools in the state system were now so numerous. The question arose as to what would become of the school buildings and this coincided with a desire on the part of several people to establish a hospice in the city. About that time Sue Ryder decided to set up a similar hospice in

Leeds and it looked as though the two were going to be in competition for local authority support. So, I called together a meeting between the Sue Ryder people and the Cross and Passion nuns to see if they couldn't effect a common purpose. It failed because their approaches were considerably different and they both decided to go their own way. This created great financial difficulties and these have remained. Anyway, both went ahead and I have been friendly with both places. I knew Sue Ryder and I sometimes visited Wheatfield's, the Sue Ryder home, as well as St Gemma's.

In 1977 I was among the speakers at an open meeting in Leeds Town Hall which launched the appeal fund for St Gemma's Hospice. Also there were members of the medical profession, the Cross and Passion sisters together with Anglican, Free Church and Jewish representatives. Happily it was possible to open St Gemma's Hospice in the following year. Three years later the first purpose built accommodation was completed and to mark the occasion I presented the hospice with a bronze bust of St Gemma sculpted by my old friend, Dr Arthur Fleischmann.

The official opening of the new building at St Gemma's in 1982 was performed by the Prince and Princess of Wales. It was a great occasion when they came to visit the hospice and the patients who were already there. On the day it was my duty to welcome them to St Gemma's. I discovered shortly beforehand in looking at the history of the Cross and Passion nuns that the Order might not have come into existence more than a century ago without the rule of life drawn up for them by a holy Passionist Father, who was a very notable convert. His name was Ignatius Spencer. And he is a great, great, great uncle of the Princess of Wales! I was able, therefore, to point out to her that we might not have been there at all on that day if the Cross and Passion order had not been brought together, so to speak, by Father Ignatius Spencer. Her presence was singularly appropriate and greatly appreciated. Both Prince and Princess spent a long time talking with the patients who were there: so much so that they over ran their time by an hour and the Lord Lieutenant was getting more and more concerned about their engagements. Anyway, it all went off well and has lasting memories for everyone associated with St Gemma's. The Duke and Duchess of Norfolk also have played a great part in the venture because of their experience in similar hospices in the South. Altogether the

Hospice Movement has firmly taken root in the Diocese not only in Leeds but subsequently in other areas as well. I remember, for example, having a good deal to do with one in Halifax which is very thriving nowadays. Such centres also play a very big part in the ecumenical life of the areas as they receive generous support from Catholics and non-Catholics alike.

The Clarke-Foley Bequest arose out of an extraordinary experience when a gentleman from America, James Clarke, came to see me at Bishop's House. He arrived in a giant Cadillac motor car and wearing a Stetson hat; both were rather unusual sights in Thorner. He came to ask me if he and his sister, (his sister was a widow and he was a bachelor), could leave the bulk of their money to somebody like the Bishop of a Diocese who would undertake to apply it as far as possible to the needs of old people in the area in which they had lived as children. The Clarkes had originally migrated from Ireland in the time of the famine to Addingham, near Ilkley. They were very devoted Catholics, and as children they used to walk barefooted to the Catholic school in Ilkley. Now they wanted something to be done for the old people of that area. So when they both ultimately died they left their money to the Diocese for me to administer. I decided from the start that it would be important to do this as far as possible ecumenically. I had discovered that what was very much wanted in the Ilkley area was a day centre for the aged. The town had been hoping to do something about it but hadn't got the money to do it. I realised that it was no use starting a place like that unless there was local support to fund its running costs once it was built. We, therefore, got all the different organisations concerned with the elderly in that area together and put it to them that we would pay for the place to be built if they would all undertake to play their part in it. Their agreement enabled the Clarke-Foley Centre to be built and since 1981 it has become a very successful centre for the town's old people, and is a very fine building.

Once that had been done it was left to me to decide what else would be done with the bequest. A considerable amount of money was also available for other old people's groups in the area. For example in Addingham itself a trust fund of £50,000 was set up to benefit the aged. They didn't need a building as they had a very nice hall. But they wanted to be able to make greater use of it for their local people and to be able to lay on various facilities for them which were impossible otherwise. So that was done. I also gave some money to Wood Hall and something towards the refurbishment of the Sacred Heart Church in Ilkley. When this work was completed in late 1979 the church became a memorial to James Clarke and Sarah Foley.

In some respects a diocesan bishop acts as the Church's ambassador or representative to the wider community, especially on important civic or social occasions. Do any events of this kind stand out from your time in Leeds?

One event I shall always remember happened in 1977, when I was invited to dinner on board the Royal Yacht. I still have the menu from that occasion, and the day was the 13th July 1977. 'It was the year that the Queen celebrated her Silver Jubilee and during her visit to Yorkshire she hosted several gatherings in different places. You can imagine my surprise when I was invited to dinner on the Royal Yacht, *Britannia*, in the King George V dock in Hull. For me it was a most memorable occasion. The only other cleric beside myself was the Archbishop of York, who was there with his wife; many other distinguished people from the whole of Yorkshire were also present. When we arrived and went on board, we were greeted by the Duchess of Grafton and afterwards were all presented to Her Majesty the Queen and the Duke of Edinburgh. Dinner followed in the ship's dining room. There were fifty guests and a band played in the distance all the way through the meal but did not interfere with the conversation. Afterwards we went back into the main lounge of the ship, but as we went out of the dining room I was somewhat puzzled because a young lady came up to me and said "I am so glad you are here tonight." I said "Well, I am sure that I am very glad that you are here. Why are you so glad that I am here?" And she replied "Well don't you realise if you hadn't have been here, I wouldn't have been here." I said "What do you mean?" She said "Well you see there are twenty-four married couples here tonight as far as I can make out and you and me. I hope that explains it. I shall be devoted to clerical celibacy all the rest of my life!" It turned out that she was the daughter of one of the Lord Lieutenants who were present; her father and mother were there and because I hadn't got a Mrs she was invited also. Afterwards we went up on deck for the Beating of the Retreat and altogether it was a very lovely occasion. Another thing that I remember especially about that evening was a notice right opposite the gangway which the Queen ascended to board the ship; instead of saying "Welcome to Humberside" it said "Welcome to the East Riding of Yorkshire". I feel sure that the Queen must have been interested in that.

On another occasion I had to make a speech thanking the Duke of Edinburgh for coming to Trinity and All Saints' College in Leeds, and for his remarks about how well planned the college was. I told him of an incident regarding planning which happened when I was interviewing students for the priesthood. One boy came forward and I asked him how many brothers and sisters he had and he said "Twelve", and I said with some compassion in my voice "What does your father do for a living?" "My father," he said, "is an expert in planning and production."

A Bishop remains ever a priest and despite the various responsibilities which come with episcopacy, prayer must remain an important, if not central feature of one's life. What are your own thoughts on the role of prayer in priestly life?

I am glad you said that a Bishop has got always to remember that he is a priest. I can remember after I was first consecrated I was concelebrating Mass in Hull, one of the first concelebrations that were celebrated in the light of the decree on the liturgy from Vatican II. One layman came up to a priest friend of mine and said to him "Was that the Bishop in the middle of that crowd at Mass?" and he said "Yes". "How remarkable," he replied "I thought they gave up that sort of thing when they became Bishops". And I can remember about the same time making a thanksgiving after Mass in a church, also in Hull, when an altar boy went by into the Sacristy where the parish priest was putting out the vestments for the next Mass. The boy apparently said to him: "Is that the Bishop in the church?" And the parish priest said "Yes it is". He said "Does it say Mass like a priest?"

I would like to make it quite clear before talking about the influence of the Church on my prayer life that I do owe a great debt to my upbringing. Faithfulness to prayer was taken for granted. For example, in my grandfather's household we had family prayers at the beginning of the day, and everybody was brought into them. There was a cowherd called David who was always grumbling to my grandfather about this, that or the other. We were all kneeling there and my grandfather led the psalm

"Lord remember David and all his afflictions" and I can remember having to control myself very strongly not to burst out into laughter. But there was that sort of atmosphere in the home and I found myself even as quite a small boy saying prayers and asking for God's protection. It was primarily intercession: but at church it took on a worshipping aspect. Later on there were confirmation classes and retreats. I loved the Authorised Version of the Bible and read it daily. Indeed I had been brought up not only on the Gospels but all the lovely stories of the Old Testament. At Oxford I discovered some of the spiritual classics. I tried to follow some of their inspirations. But one didn't always find it very easy. In my own experience I resorted more to prayer in the days when I was a schoolmaster and Chaplain at Lancing than at other times in my pre-Catholic days. This was because I felt very strongly that I needed God's help in teaching religion throughout the school to these young men and boys. I found myself giving more time to it and trying to understand more fully what it meant to make progress at prayer. One of the things that happened was that it became very clear to me that I must become a Catholic.

When I went to the Beda College in Rome I found that we had to be up, every morning very early, at 5.30am and in the chapel at 6.00am. We were all there for silent prayer or meditation, as it was called. It was followed by the Mass and Thanksgiving before we thought of breakfast and the lectures of the day. Indeed the whole of one's life at the college was interspersed with prayer: not only spiritual reading and meditation and the daily Mass but also visits to the chapel at various times, and the saying of evening prayer communally. There was also the rosary together and the para-liturgical events which are in a sense the background of true priestly life. To me all this was a very great help because one learnt more about prayer and tried to understand some of the ways in which there could be progress at prayer. We learnt that we were to try to love Our Lord more. In this regard, prayer before the Blessed Sacrament in which He is Himself present in all our Churches, was a very great focus and has remained so to me all my life as I think it does to all priests and great numbers of the laity. This special love for Jesus the second person of the Blessed Trinity who became man for our Salvation leads us also to the other Persons of the Godhead: through Jesus Christ Our Lord, to the Father in the Holy Spirit. One was indeed very grateful for the pattern of life that was given to us in the Seminary of those days.

Today I understand there is much greater freedom of development which doesn't always have the same effect, because of human nature being what it is. When you had to be there for certain times and you obeyed bells, you went. But when you are left to organise your own spiritual life it doesn't always go with such regularity and therefore I have ever been encouraging both the priests and the students to do everything they can to be radically faithful to their own times of prayer. Of course the whole purpose of what happens now in the Seminaries is supposed to be a development and enrichment and can be an enrichment if a man really organises himself, and this becomes lasting. But if he doesn't he is going to be at a great loss. This remains the fundamental and most important thing of a priest's life, and of a bishop's life: that he is faithful to those times spent alone with God.

You may ask what he is to do in those times? Well all the great spiritual classics make it clear that to begin with the general pattern is that of meditating on the Gospels especially, but also on the Scriptures in general. In a lesser way much help may be forthcoming from the spiritual masterpieces of all the ages. But the real process is something that is much more personal than that because for every Christian it should be a closer love and devotion to God through Jesus Christ Our Lord. Now if you love a person you don't just want to be thinking about them, you don't even want to be talking to them all the time, you want to be listening, yes, to what they have to say. But also you share silence together. This is a fundamental test of genuine friendship. It is also a very important ingredient of progress in prayer. Indeed the spiritual writers say that as you make a certain progress in prayer you are reduced to saying less than you did when you meditated. Maybe now you utter brief prayers from the heart rather than the mind: short ejaculations like "My God, I love you" interspersed with periods of silence. This in its turn leads on to longer periods of silence, and a listening rather than speaking. I have met people who are well advanced in prayer, who can just "switch off" for a few minutes or half-an-hour; just basking in the presence of God, but also for long periods in the darkness of his seeming "absence". The whole of our life is determined by God. He sustains us at every moment of our being and we must have this love for Him which comes from our approach through Jesus Christ, Our Lord, who is God made man. Nevertheless at times we are going to find it very difficult to pray. There will be times of innumerable distractions and feelings of absolute frustration and a failure to make any progress. But there is an old saying that nobody is a judge in his own cause. And so, one should never be put off by this. In fact it can be a period of the greatest progress. So we must have courage. And sometimes we need a wise counsellor.

Another great obstacle to growth in prayer is sin. For sin cuts us off from God and, therefore, it is very difficult for a sinner to pray. But he should and he must go on saying "God have mercy on me a sinner" like the publican, as against the Pharisee, in the parable. We must all rise again very quickly from sin. Frequent confession will help here. Prayer, as one gradually learns, is something as essential as oxygen and it is more essential than anything else in the life of a priest. And not only of priests because this could happen to anyone who is not a priest. It could happen to anyone who is baptised, even to the non-baptised because God has created them all. And there is such a thing as the desire of Faith with which they are credited if they have never heard the Gospel. So the infinite love of God is something that surpasses all knowledge. Therefore, I think it is very important that people should be guided in prayer. There are certain stages that they reach in prayer when they feel they are doing nothing and they want to go back to the first stage. This is generally speaking wrong, but they need encouragement just to go on. Now I would say that in the priesthood this is more important than anything else. It can have the widest effect on the diocese, on the parish and even when things seem to be going wildly wrong in the whole life of the Church it can be bringing something about according to God's mind. But remember it isn't our doing. It is His doing. It is letting Him take over and that is extremely important. I would think, therefore, the most important thing in any priest's or bishop's life is that he has been faithful and continues to be faithful to the times of prayer and the more he does it, the more he will want to do it and the more time he will want to give to it. This can perhaps only have happened for some when they are passing into retirement. But all the same there should be a great priority given to this, even in the most momentous and busy life. And remember that the greatest thing is not efficiency but allowing God to take over. I have often been helped by some of the wise maxims of Abbot Chapman in his *Spiritual Letters*: such as "Pray as you can and don't try to pray as you can't". And "the less time you give to it the worse it becomes".

There is real progress in an approach of simplicity and the relinquishing of all complications. When the disciples asked their Master to teach them to pray, you know the answer that He gave. Prayer is a personal relationship with the Father.

In the summer of 1985 you retired as Bishop of Leeds shortly after your seventy-fifth birthday. In the light of your own experience, gained during the previous twenty-one years, how do you see the role of a Bishop in relation to his people and also in relation to the rest of the Church?

Vatican II's Decree on the Pastoral Office of Bishops in the Church says quite simply that the Bishops, as the successors of the Apostles, are commissioned to perpetuate the work of Christ the eternal pastor. That means that they are empowered to teach, to sanctify and to give spiritual nourishment to their priests who share so much with them in the Sacrament of Holy Order. As Fathers and Pastors they should be with all their people as those 'who serve'. They must show compassion and love. They must ever be aware of the needs of their priests and people. The various forms of the apostolate must be encouraged. Each diocese is in its way a microcosm of the Universal Church. It will need certain structure to strengthen its unity; but at the same time it should abhor bureaucracy. In all things the Christ-pattern of the Good Shepherd is to be followed.

It is important for the Bishop to do his utmost to give an example of prayer and a loving relationship with the Successor of St Peter, who is there in a special God-given way to 'confirm' his brethren. He will count too on a close relationship with his fellow-bishops, his priests and all his people. For, as John Paul II said at Westminster to the Bishops of England and Wales: "You are never alone." We all share in the Universality of God's Church and these relationships are fundamental. God's power for all His people finds its full scope in weakness. Of ourselves we are nothing: but with Christ we can do all things. Ultimately He uses the simple to confound the wise. A Bishop always has the consolation that he could never have become one unless God's Church had called him. The onus never rests just on himself. He can always say "Make me a channel of your Peace, dear God."

When the time came, in 1985, how did you feel about the prospect of retirement?

Many people nowadays greet me with the question: "How are you enjoying your retirement?" In 1985, when I was about to retire, having reached my 75th year, a lady in Bradford wished me a happy redundancy!

I must admit that for a short time I found it something of a traumatic experience. Looking back I think this was because Catholic bishops usually died in harness and until the new Canon Law appeared in the early eighties there was nothing very definite about it. Section one of Canon 401 now reads as follows: 'A diocesan Bishop who has completed his 75th year of age is requested to offer his resignation from office to the Supreme Pontiff, who, taking all the circumstances into account, will make provision accordingly.'

Of course, this is a very sensible piece of legislation. And in future all bishops will come to terms, over a long period, with the idea of ultimate retirement and perhaps even decide how and where they will spend it. Together with my own contemporaries the possibility of 'coming to terms' with it had been very brief. And our lives as diocesan bishops were so demanding that there was neither time nor inclination to think much about it.

In my own case there was another complication. All my years of Priesthood had been spent in the Archdiocese of Westminster. As a Bishop I belonged to the Diocese of Middlesbrough before being translated to Leeds. In which of these three should I retire? There were other questions also, I had lived for many years of my life in Lancashire and in Sussex as well as London and Yorkshire. I have many contacts in all of these places. Furthermore, I had not decided how I wished to spend my retirement. It could be that I should seek to live within or near to a Benedictine monastery such as Downside or Ampleforth. I had many different, kind suggestions made to me. So at the moment of my retirement in September 1985 the only thing clear to me was that I must give time to thinking out the choices that lay before me and to asking the Good Lord to guide me.

I sometimes refer to the next three months as "my voluntary exile". I drove off in the first instance to Sussex. I stayed with various friends and relations there and elsewhere. And ultimately I went to Downside Abbey for a sort of Retreat to get things clear with the help of God. Despite the loving kindness of so many people I felt like a shepherd who had lost all his sheep. My heart was longing for the Yorkshire people and their beloved countryside: my roots for the last quarter of a century and indeed my roots by birth. Was this quite irrational? Gradually all the alternatives seemed to raise other problems rather than providing a clear solution. So I had to get down to sorting out exactly the kind of retirement I envisaged.

Downside was a good rendezvous for such discourses. And the Abbot helped me greatly in our conversations. I had remembered the saying of a venerable Carthusian monk that retirement for a priest must spell progress and not deterioration. He had reminded me that many medieval bishops, for example, thought it *de riguer* 'to make their soul' in some quiet retreat before they died, in some reparation for their sins and mistakes, and failures, as well as to intercede for the greater well-being, in the eyes of God, for their diocese and people: thus benefiting the Universal Church. All those thoughts should surely appeal today to those who are only too aware of their inadequacies. At the same time one must be realistic. It is not easy for a monastery nowadays to take on an old man as a kind of postulant, physically and otherwise. And if he was to live in a cottage in the precincts he would probably need a housekeeper or at least somebody to look after him. In these days such acquisitions are at a premium.

I then began to think of retirement with a Religious Order of men or women whose special calling it is to look after the elderly. I had hoped from the beginning to retire somewhere that would surround one with a frame-work of liturgical life, with opportunity for reading and perhaps writing, with daily Mass and a certain freedom whereby one could still carry on some kind of apostolate. At the same time it would have to be a community that could bring one into its infirmary on becoming less independent and perhaps more 'gaga' than at present.

At this point I began to consider a suggestion that had kindly been made to me by the Provincial in this country of the Little Sisters of the Poor. She had spoken of a small flat in the College of the Blessed Virgin Mary at Headingley in Leeds. Very soon it seemed to be a providential answer to all my needs. My only reservation was that I did not want in any way to be an embarrassment to my successor. When I discussed this with the Abbot at Downside he pointed out that at least three of my contemporaries had already retired in similar institutions in their own former dioceses and that it seemed to be working all right. Accordingly, I wrote a long letter to Bishop David Konstant in Leeds asking him what he thought. I made it clear that I would always want to keep a low profile. He replied by return of post. "No problem" and "welcome". He has ever been most kind, generous and thoughtful on my behalf and I owe him my deepest gratitude.

So I came to the Little Sisters of the Poor whom I knew well of old; and from my point of view it has made my retirement a very happy one and also one in which I have been kept fully occupied in sharing to some extent their life, to read; it allows me to write, to visit, to listen to beautiful music, and still to play a useful part I hope in the life of the Church in this diocese and elsewhere, preaching and saying Mass, confirming, lecturing and corresponding with a host of old friends here and there at home and abroad. I am still able to travel at home and abroad and able to drive myself about in this lovely countryside.

Happily, retired Bishops are kept in touch with the Universal Church, receiving through the Apostolic Nunciature all the documents of the Holy See. Similarly, the National Conference of English and Welsh Hierarchy, welcome us to all their deliberations as often as we wish, and supply us with all the usual information produced by the Secretariat, and this helps us to feel very much a part of our Mother the Church.

THE SHAPE OF THINGS TO COME?

My Lord, I think you would agree with me, given your interest in history, that we cannot hope to understand the present, nor the likely trend of future developments, without reflecting on the past. As we look ahead to the 'shape of things to come', can you see any parallels between our own times and a previous era in the Church's history?

Indeed I can and as I think about these matters I am reminded of an event which took place in 1946. On the 1st May that year the mortal remains of Bishop Richard Challoner were brought to Westminster Cathedral from the tomb of the Barrett family at Milton. It was an extraordinary event because this holy Vicar Apostolic of the London District had never received Catholic burial on account of the times in which he died, following the Gordon riots. After his body had been removed from the coffin it was transferred into a new inner and outer coffin and the remains were identified in the presence of the whole Hierarchy of England and Wales. Richard Challoner was a very holy man and it seems strange that nothing has happened in regard to the promotion of his cause. For on the occasion described above he received Catholic burial, again in the presence of the Hierarchy, in the Chapel of St Gregory and the English Saints. There were many on that occasion who thought they would live to see his Beatification and ultimate Canonisation. This has not happened and many think the explanation in the providence of God is that Bishop Richard Challoner, who had done so much to record the lives of the martyrs himself, would certainly have wanted, as Newman would have wanted, those men to be raised first to the altars of the Church before any thought be given regarding English Confessors of a later period.

I have a feeling that the time is now coming when the cause of Richard Challoner will go forward, in the way that the Newman cause is progressing. And my reason is this: Challoner lived through some of the most difficult and depressing days of English Catholicism since the Reformation. In the 18th Century when he was the Vicar Apostolic of the London District, Catholic life in this country reached its lowest ebb. He might well have been depressed and discouraged by the apostasy of the owners of so many of the Great Catholic houses which afforded the facilities of Mass and the Sacraments to the ordinary laity in different parts of the country. It often looked as though the life of the Church in this country was collapsing altogether. But whenever Richard Challoner was challenged about this he made one consistent response: "There will be a new people". As we know, this really was quite prophetic because there followed, very soon after his death, the great emigrations from France to our country of priests, especially of religious, on account of the French Revolution. There was to follow the vast influx of people from Ireland due to the potato famine in the middle of the 19th century. And there was to be another addition to the 'new people' by the throng of converts following the example of Newman and Manning (all of whom were going to play their part together with the devoted Catholic remnant in the great Revival of the 'Second Spring'). So, it seems to me that the remark of his successor Bishop Milner at the time of Challoner's funeral, that this man would one day be canonised, should have a promise of truth about it. Indeed it is one of those historic phases where there is surely a parallel between some of the trials that Richard Challoner endured, and those of our own age: with defections and a decline of the birth rate leading to pessimism in many quarters.

I have begun by drawing attention to the Challoner period because I think it is relevant to our time that we need always as Christians and as Catholics to be optimistic and to have the confidence that God's Church is never ultimately going to fail. Indeed, the contrary is true, the contrary is promised and I would say again that "there will be a new people". But if you ask me who and what these new people are going to be, it is not easy to give any cut and dried answer because it will all happen according to the providence of God. There are, however, certain signs of the kind of ways in which there could be a new people. We know first of all, don't we, that from the start there has got to be in our time a real renewal and it is this that the Second Vatican Council has tried to bring into the increasingly secular societies of modern Europe. It is very important that great notice should be taken of this because there could be here a very clear sign of the shape of things to come. The new people are surely going to be the People of God of *Lumen Gentium*, a new and fuller presence of Church in our world: 'The Living Stones'.

There will doubtless be other elements as well; but this is going to play a very considerable part. It is all going to be connected to my mind with the new responsibilities in the whole life of the Church regarding the laity. The lead has already been given by Pope John Paul II in his magnificent Apostolic Exhortation on The Vocation and Mission of the Lay Faithful in the Church and in the World. This is something which is going to enrich the whole life of the Church in the world generally and especially in our continent of Europe. And I believe it will have a great formative influence. Take, for example, the Rite of Christian Initiation of Adults (RCIA) which is playing, despite its name, a very large part in all catechesis. There seems to be emerging, a very interesting return to the processes of the early Church in informing people about the Catholic Faith and enabling them to progress in understanding the meaning of 'Church'.

To sum up, what I am saying is that I feel sure that the shape of things to come is a shape which is very like that which succeeded the dark and dreary and extremely trying days of the 18th century, from the Catholic point of view, ending up in the Gordon Riots. That must have seemed the final destruction of everything: London lost even its Embassy Chapels that were so dear to Richard Challoner. But despite all he never lost his faith that there would be a 'new people' and I am sure this will be true for us also.

God's ways are not our ways. And He holds the whole world in the palm of His hands. Many people are beginning to realise this in the extraordinary and entirely unpredictable events that have happened recently in Russia and Eastern Europe. And there are signs of a new return to the Christian roots which created our civilisation.

Does the need for this 'new people' suggest that Britain has ceased to be a Christian country?

Some years ago one would have said 'no' but the situation has greatly changed in the 60s, 70s, and 80s, I think. I remember an international evangelist from Australia coming and speaking to us at the house of the Bishop of Bradford a few years ago. He was not a Catholic but he said something like this: "Your country is really in a deplorable state from the point of view of Christianity: far worse that any other English-speaking country. Even materialistic America has a far higher percentage of worshipping people. The whole of this country needs re-evangelising. It has departed so far from the worship of God, from the Scriptures, from the moral code of Christianity that it is really very lamentable and, of course, we are all very conscious that some of the thinking of government nowadays especially with the kind of legislation that has made abortion permissible, has really gone against the whole Christian tradition of a country, whose law was founded on Christian principles. Now you are drifting away from the Christendom you used to proclaim." I have quoted this on many occasions and I think it is very humiliating to think that our country has gone so far.

Having said that one must be quite clear that there are a lot of very good people and a lot of very loving people and a lot of very committed people but they are not making their weight felt and one of the most important things in this age is to urge committed Christians to play a much greater part in politics, in local politics as well as national politics, but also in the Trade Unions and all the other organisations in which the laity alone can influence our country's life. Please God the new age of the laity will help to alter all this. We have got fewer Christian inspired people working today in all the different facets of society and culture than was the case even in the not too distant past. Again it makes me think of the 18th Century and the new hope that must be ours with regard to the future.

Of course, I may be wrong if I give the impression that the 'new' people will be ourselves 'renewed'; I hope, however, that we may have the grace to play our part. But Almighty God may have other plans of missionising our country anew from Africa, India, South America or elsewhere. The decline of Christianity here and in the western world generally is alarming and is not only a departure from the faith but also from the moral teachings of Christianity. This is a dominant challenge to return to the law, the commandments and the love of God which is the solemn teaching of the Church through the ages. And that is the only way of turning our country away from the **national suicide** which is also unwittingly being pursued by some other nations as well as in Europe and America.

It is quite clear that there has got to be a new evangelisation of our country and the whole question of the ecumenical scene, to my mind, is connected with this. One of the main reasons for ecumenism that is put forward in the Vatican Decree is that it is an obstacle and scandal to the world of our time that Christians are divided and we need more and more to speak with a common voice. Of course, that in itself isn't a sufficient reason for unity. The main reason for unity is that it is the will of God that it should happen as we know from the prayer of Christ in the Gospel. He wanted us to be one and He prayed that we should be one and this oneness has got to be promoted. Therefore, every possible work must be done to bring about organic Christian Unity. I say 'organic' Christian Unity because it is no use just having an intercommunion without a realisation of the whole meaning of 'Church'. Ecclesiology makes it essential that there should be a oneness in structure and that can never happen if people try to bypass that fact. Inter-communion will be the joyful gift of unity achieved and it is a disservice to the whole of ecumenical work to try to by-pass and force an issue. There must be a growing together in the understanding of fundamental truth, of the mind of Christ in doctrine and morality, as well as the performance of common works of mercy together. At the same time unity can enhance variety based on fundamental agreements. In that sense, unity does not always mean uniformity. There has always been a richness of different traditions in the Church's life.

So far I have been speaking entirely in terms of Christian unity but in our country now there are many other religions, the Muslims and the Sikhs, for example and others. I think one of the most impressive events of the last few years was when Pope John Paul II called together in Assisi religious leaders from all over the world to pray together and he did that because of the recognition which we must all have, that people of other faiths share with us the very important fundamental of belief in God. Whilst it is very difficult for us to find any common ground for uniting apart from that, this is after all an essential start. The Pope was very careful when he went to Assisi to see that the Christian prayer which has always been, as you know, through Jesus Christ Our Lord in the Holy Spirit to the Father, is something quite apart from the prayer of the non-Christian voice which is directly and solely to a single person, the Godhead. Nevertheless, there seems to be every reason why we should bring these others with us to bear witness to the need, first of all for the worship of God, because we all have that in common and secondly, because of the necessity of a common morality, in so far as this is obtainable. With regard to the first of those things, I have often quoted the saying of

Harold MacMillan that things began to go wrong in our country when people ceased to worship God. The worship of God is not only a solemn duty but is also one that leads to men's ultimate perfection and maturity. The need to exercise it communally and individually is implanted in every man and woman throughout the world. Therefore, many of those groups of people who are non-Christians can be a very great example to us in this respect in that they have a realisation that worship isn't just an act of adoration to God. It is that, of course, primarily, but in the second place it is an enrichment of the maturity of the person. There is a lot of nonsense talked about maturity nowadays, about people having reached a degree of maturity. I don't believe myself that anyone reaches full maturity until they get to Heaven. And by that I mean Heaven because real maturity has got to be an absolute fullness. That does not, however, impede a start from being made. It is something essential to the whole of human nature that things are never going to be right again until the duty of worship has been restored. This has obviously important consequences for all evangelisation. Clearly this widens the whole picture of the ecumenical field.

A lot has been done and said regarding Christian ecumenism, the unity of Christians. On all levels there has been a dialogue. In our own country there has been a remarkable dialogue, known as the ARCIC event where a certain amount of agreement has been made between the Catholic Church and the Anglican Church. There is a great danger that an agreement of that kind and on that level will ever be so remote from ordinary people that it is not going to achieve the unity in itself. It is an important approach but there have been similar important approaches in history. For example, at the Council of Florence in the 15th Century there was an agreement between the eastern and the western churches that the Filioque clause of the Creed and other problems would be settled and that there would be a restoration of unity that had broken three centuries previously. But because it never penetrated to the ordinary people it never happened. The same thing could happen here if dialogue on all levels is not promoted. More and more there seems to be an emphasis on the local level which has a great deal to be said for it and one hopes that this will continue. There are, however, a lot of people nowadays who think that no progress has been made and that we might as well go back to our divisions. The whole idea of ecumenism is that the different divisions can enrich one another in preparing the way for unity but it would be very defeatist to go back to the kind of intolerance that has happened in the past. How can we guard against this? To me it seems that there is only one very clear way of guarding against it and that is by joining together in a common evangelisation of a country that has become very largely pagan. And so, one wants to see somebody drawing up the kind of principles wherein all these different bodies both of Christians and of non-Christians can play a part in the kind of evangelisation that will overpower the growth of paganism and restore the true spirit ultimately of Christianity. How is this to be done?

These are matters which you touched upon towards the end of an address which you gave at the 50th anniversary of Moral Re-Armament in October, 1988. Could you perhaps reiterate those comments in the light of the Church's approach to the dawn of the third millennium?

You rightly point out that I spoke on this very subject in St Margaret's, Westminster in October 1988 and if I may quote something that I said there I think it would elucidate what I mean by joint Christian Evangelisation. "Many surprising things of great promise are happening in the world today as we approach the third millennium. By God's Grace we shall continue to play some part in the healing of conflicts on all levels. There are many outstanding followers of the Moral Re-Armament Movement who will play a part in the economic and social side of humanity's development. This is happening now and will doubtless continue. May the numbers of these dedicated men and women increase. The Christian reclaiming of the Western World, as you well know, is something especially dear to the mind and heart of Pope John Paul II who by his great spiritual and pastoral example proclaims so tirelessly the message of Christ in all its entirety. It is thought that the task is so vast that it needs the fullest co-operation of all committed Christians and others by their prayer and activity; and that such ecumenical evangelism could lead us closer to Christian Unity which today seems in some ways so remote. In this regard, Moral Re-Armament enriched by the wisdom of its 50 years may surely be pointing the way. For the simple message of the four Absolutes: honesty, purity, selflessness, and love, those four 'mighty pillars', presented as always in the light of Christ can provide us with a common front already tried. And can it not lead us to an even greater unity in striving together to 'remake the world'."

You see, Moral Re-Armament is not in itself a religion, it is acceptable to all forms of Christianity and to people of non-Christian faiths from many parts of the world, but who subscribe in the light of their own faith to those four absolutes of absolute honesty, absolute purity, absolute selflessness and absolute love.

I can remember a Benedictine Abbot in Rome saying "Moral Rearmament can win all men because its standards are universally valid. It is not in itself a religion nor a substitute for religion. It is not a sect. It has four mighty pillars upon which human living must be based. Everyone must accept these ideas if he is honest with himself". And later on Cardinal Koenig emphasised this when he said "I believe that a discovery which the founder of Moral Rearmament made in this area will prove to be correct. That people in the east as well as the west need the courage to look deep inside themselves and to discover the conscience that our creator has implanted in every one of us. In other words the source of spirit and truth". To me this thinking is of great importance for now and for the future for all men and women of all nations are made in the image of God. In other words there is a divine spark in all of us. Sometimes it is not easy to find it but it is there because God Himself made it so. A divine mechanism, if you like, which has moved many dear friends of ours, men and women of many faiths who want to help bring God's kingdom on earth. We have met with such people and indeed this commitment to God's kingdom to a world He made is one that is total in concept and so we are enriched by the presence of these non-Christians. We must only hope that they too are enriched by our Christian presence and perhaps perceive something of the sublime mysteries of incarnation and redemption which bring new light and new promise to the coming of God's kingdom. It is said that "the world today does not condemn us for being Christians but for not being Christian enough". Those last words came from the mouth of another Cardinal, Cardinal Suenens, when he was speaking to some of the Charismatic groups.

As we approach this third millennium we can be filled with hope and hope is one of three great virtues: faith, hope and love. With the growth of hope there should be equally a growth of faith as well as a growth of love. These things are a kind of trinity in themselves and a kind of unity. The human person is so made by his very nature that he is fundamentally a religious person. He has a divine spark within him and this divine spark needs to be developed into a greater maturity. Therefore, we should ever be concerned about the process of showing people the real meaning of their humanity and that is one of the things in which the Holy Father, Pope John Paul II has excelled himself from the first encyclical of his pontificate. I would like to think that the more that mankind realises the dignity of its vocation and of the human person, the more it will aspire to be something even more wonderful in the Christian concept of Jesus Christ. I would think, therefore, that all attempts to present a united front which will concentrate on the idea of the new world that we need to create, the fundamental principles that we need to inject, can lead not only to a transformation of mankind in the third millennium but also can dispose us to be the recipients of God's infinite mercy. There is always a danger of the heresy of Pelagianism which fundamentally is thinking we can do everything ourselves and that we have no need of any supernatural support. This is extremely dangerous and against all Christian thinking. The scriptures tell us that Christ says "Without me you can do nothing", but St Paul says "With Christ I can do all things." Let us not think for a moment that we are going to be left without many graces from the Godhead in approaching this new millennium and we should have great confidence. This confidence will be intensified in so far as we become right now a 'new people' dedicated to Him and to the coming of His kingdom.

The amazing events in the Soviet Union and the countries of Eastern Europe which have taken place since 1989 show us how God can bring about events surpassing our wildest dreams. The euphoria will pass and great problems of transition will arise. These will be a great challenge to the Christian conscience. God give us the hearts and minds and leadership to respond with deep dedication and compassion and thus rediscover the fundamental roots of our Christian civilisation.

EPILOGUE

I was brought up to love the Scriptures. At Oxford in the early thirties the Honours School of Theology, instead of deepening that love had the opposite effect because of its preoccupation with German Higher Criticism. It seemed to me totally destructive, and it took me many years to rediscover the glories of the Old and New Testaments. In this I was greatly helped by becoming a Catholic. The new Biblical movements in the Catholic Church, especially in the Pontificate of Pope Pius XII, established a reassuring balance and the Second Vatican Council spoke out loud and clear for the wider promulgation of the Word of God in all its aspects. The riches that have ensued for the whole life of the Church are beyond all computation. This, together with the pastoral aspects of the Second Vatican Council whereby the whole People of God were brought ever more fully into the Church's life, is for me the supreme fruit of the Conciliar event. And so one's deep love and gratitude for Bible and for Church is ever increasing.

In this context the Second Vatican Council's documents deserve study and are often deeply revealing. This I think is especially true of **Lumen Gentium**, the great Constitution on the Church which evolved in its final form over a comparatively long period of prayer and discussion. Jesus Christ, the second Person of the Blessed Trinity made man, our Redeemer and Saviour established His Church to apply His achievement to subsequent generations. Together with the Father He sent the Third Person, the Spirit of their love, to be the principle of its life and to lead us into all Truth. Although a Divine institution, His Church was to have a human componency. Yet it was to be His mystical Body. It would have its visual aid so to speak in the Risen Lord. But it was also to be given a visual aid of what it ultimately would become on the purely human level and this is what happened in the famous eighth chapter of **Lumen Gentium** on the Blessed Virgin Mary.

Originally it had been intended to have a totally independent document on the Virgin Mother. Some of the Fathers of the Council were at first outraged when it was propounded that instead of such a tribute to the Mother of God she was to be given one chapter in the document on the Church. They came gradually to see, doubtless under the inspiration of the Holy Spirit, that if this was done the role of Mary, far from being diminished would be greatly enhanced and at the same time made much more comprehensible to non-Catholics.

But there was much more to be understood from it than just that. The Early Fathers of the Church had repeatedly spoken of Mary's role as a model of what Christ's Church would ultimately become. This connotation, far from being new, belonged to the whole tradition of Patristic studies in both East and West. Moreover it pointed the way to new Scriptural investigations regarding the Marian texts, especially in the New Testament, which more than ever began to justify the entire Catholic and Orthodox tradition of the Church's teaching on the Virgin Mother. How interesting it was to find this wonderful new enrichment in the Holy Father's encyclical for the Marian Year particularly on the texts of the Visitation and the Presentation in the Temple as well as at Calvary, regarding the Marian vocation to show the way of Christian participation in union with the achievement of the Sole Redeemer.

There is no happier note on which I would end these memoirs. My love of the Blessed Virgin began in Walsingham long before I became a Catholic. When I was a student in Rome her message and her role developed for me in theology and in prayer. When Cardinal Hinsley ordained me priest I went at once to the Slipper Chapel at Walsingham to say my first Mass. Since those days I have come to know her and love her at many of her shrines. And as you can imagine it gave me great joy to have the task of setting up her new shrine in Westminster Cathedral. Diocesan Pilgrimages to Lourdes, Fatima and to Our Lady of Unfailing Help in Rome have been a further enrichment.

On my ordination card in 1940 these lines appeared:

Maria Mater Gratiae	*Mary, Mother of Grace*
Dulcis Parens Clementiae	*Sweet Mother of Mercy*
Tu nos ab hoste protege	*Keep us from all evil*
Et mortis hora suscipe	*And be with us at death's hour.*

I learnt these words at Upholland in 1939. They have been on my lips ever since. And I await, in confidence, despite all my failings, the realisation of the last line of that prayer!

INDEX

Alphonso XIII of Spain 47-8
Amigo, Bishop Peter 26-7
Ampleforth Abbey 11,78-9,80,115, 138
Anrep, Boris 67
Argyll, Duke of 20
Arrowsmith, Canon Adrian 59
Arseniev, Nicolai 23

Baker, Fr. Vincent 56
Barberi, Blessed Dominic 56
Baring, Maurice 54
Barnes, Bertram 21
Barrett Family 141
Bartlett, Mgr Francis 57, 64, 67, 81
Battle, John 108
Bea, Cardinal Augustin 89
Beda College, Rome 10, 24, 33-4, 41-8, 81-2, 119
Beddes Roscoe 46
Beevor, Humphrey 19
Bell, Bishop George 10, 28
Benedict XV, Pope 62
Bentley, J.F. 63, 67
Berkeley, Sir Lennox & Lady 59
Berne, Switzerland 23-4
Bodkin, Professor 59
Borelli, Don Mario 50
Borromeo, St Charles 85
Bradford, Bishop of 143
Brighton 10, 29-30
Britten, Benjamin 69
Browne, Clara Harriet 21, 24
Brunner, Bishop George 78, 81
Buckfast Abbey 25-6, 52
Buckley, Mgr Michael 88
Burke, Fr Gerald 124
Butcher, Mgr Reginald 59
Butler, Bishop Christopher 29, 34, 35, 83

Cadman, Reginald 21
Cardinale, Archbishop Igino 11, 77, 81, 85, 90

Carlyle, Doctor A.J. 17
Carter, Ken Oliver 46
Casey, Bishop Patrick 59
Cashman, Bishop David 59, 71, 72
Chamberlain, Neville 43
Challoner, Bishop Richard 141, 142, 143
Chambers, Freddy and Pat 59
Chapman, Abbot Henry John 126
Chesterfield, 30-2
Chesterton, G.K. 98
Christie, Agatha 54
Clarke, James 131-32
Clarke, Mgr John M 61
Clarke-Foley Centre, Ilkley 131-32
Clonmore, Billy (Lord Wicklow) 19, 58
Cohen, Stanley 108
College of the B.V.M., Leeds 11, 51, 139-40
Collingwood, Mgr Cuthbert 53, 63
Collins, H.F, 14, 15
Coutourier, Abbe 91
Cowderoy, Archbishop Cyril 82
Cowgill, Bishop Joseph Robert 113
Craven, Bishop George 59, 81
Cross, Leslie 19
Cunningham, Bishop James 82

D'Arcy, Fr Martin 21-22
Davey, Fr Richard 35
Deane, Emmeline 55
Delahunt, Fr Angelus 62
Derby, Bishop of 28
Dibelius, Martin 23
Dobcross, Yorks 9
Downside Abbey 10, 34-6, 51, 52, 73, 138-9
Downside, Abbot of 139, 140
Dubois, Cardinal Louis Ernest 14
Duchemin, Mgr Charles 36, 46, 109

Dwyer, Archbishop George Patrick *85, 101, 110, 113, 115, 123*

Eastbourne *26, 27, 61*
Easton, Mrs Betty (nee Wheeler) *49*
Easton, Jack *49*
Eccles, Lancashire *9*
Edinburgh, H.R.H. Duke of *132, 133*
Edmonton, London *10, 22, 50, 60-4*
Elgar, Sir Edward *55*
'Eltofts', Bishop's House *51, 83, 113*
Elizabeth II, H.M. Queen *132, 133*
Ellesmere, Lord *9*

Felice, Archbishop Pericles *82*
Festing, Andrew *12*
Finnigan, Robert *12*
Fleischmann, Arthur & Joy *59, 130*
Foley, Sarah *131-2*
Forbes, Anne *108*
Furness, Viscount *61*

Galsworthy, John *54*
Garvin, Dr John *45*
St. Gemma's Hospice, Leeds *129-31*
Gibbs, Martin *21*
Gilbey, Mgr Alfred *63*
Godfrey, Cardinal William *34, 49, 64, 70, 71, 72*
Goebbels, Josef *43*
Goering, Hermann *43*
Gracias, Cardinal Valerian *84*
Grafton, Duchess of *132*
Grant, Bishop Charles *82, 83*
Gray, Cardinal Gordon, *90*
Green, Harry *18*
Greene, Graham *54*
Greenfield, Lancs *9*
Grensted, Rev. Dr *18, 19*
Gresham, Fr Francis *122*

Griffin, Cardinal Bernard *10, 53, 58, 60, 61, 63, 64, 68, 69, 77, 110*
Grimshaw, Archbishop Francis *85, 101*
Guazzelli, Bishop Victor *59*
Gwynn, Denis *56*

Hack, Rev Bartle *19, 20*
Halifax, Lord *43*
Hallam, Diocese of *112*
Halsey, Patrick *33*
Hankham, Sussex *9*
Harrison, Ven T. Dilworth *28, 30-32*
Hart, Donald *127-9*
Hazlewood Castle, Yorks *127-9*
Head, Francis *24*
Heenan, Cardinal John Carmel *64, 77, 98, 111, 113-14, 115*
Heim, Archbishop Bruno *54*
Heythrop College, Oxfordshire *89*
Hicks, Dom Bruno *35*
Hinsley, Cardinal Arthur *10, 36, 43, 49, 52, 58, 110, 116, 151*
Hitler, Adolf *43*
Hood, Canon Frederic *16, 19*
Houghton, Bryan *46*
Hume, Cardinal Basil *11, 38, 78, 81, 115-6*
Hyslop, Mr *14*

Ibbetson, Mrs Denise *12*
Ida, Aunt *13, 49*
Ingilby Family *126*
Ingram, Bishop Winnington *95*

Jalland, Professor *117*
James, Mgr Bruno Scott *49-51*
John XXIII, Pope *58, 75, 76, 87, 89, 120*
John Paul I, Pope *120*
John Paul II, Pope *11, 66, 103, 118, 120, 121, 122, 137, 143, 145, 147, 149*
John, Augustus *22*
Johnson, Mgr Vernon *59*

Jones, Kenneth Boulton 21
Juan Carlos, King of Spain 48

Keir, Sir David Lindsay 18
Kelly, Mgr J J 110-11
Kennedy, President John F 70-1
Kent, Duchess of 72
Kidd, Dr B.J. 20
Kilcoyne, Fr Thomas 57, 81
Kimberley Family 20
Kirk, Dr Kenneth 17, 19
Knox, Mgr Ronald 22-3, 60
Koenig, Cardinal Franz 147
Konstant, Bishop David 12, 140

Lancing College 10, 32-3, 37, 134
Leeds, Diocese of 11, 85-8, 108, 109-14, 138
Leeds, St Anne's Cathedral 12, 37, 112
Leeds University 72
Leo, XIII, Pope 40
Leys, Kenneth 18, 19
Lisieux, St Thérèse of 36, 68
Lloyd, Henry 25
London University Catholic Chaplaincy 10, 22, 50, 60-3, 64
Lucey, Bishop Cornelius 125
Lutyens, Sir Edwin 22

McCarthy, Tim 46
McGrath, Fr John George 52-54
McGuire, Mgr Peter 112
McKay, Prebendary 95
McLaughlin, Patrick 21, 24-5
MacMillan, Harold 71, 146
Madrid 48
de Maistre, Roy 68
Malcolm, George 69
Manchester Grammar School 9, 14-15
Manning, Cardinal Henry Edward 116, 142
Manzu, Giacomo 68
Mathew, Archbishop David 58
Mathew, Fr Gervase 58

Maturin, Father 30
Mawby, Colin 69
Maximus IV, Patriarch of Antioch 82
May, Lewis 56
Mercier, Cardinal Desire 20
Meyjes, Fr Walter 47-8
Middlesbrough, Diocese of 10-11, 76-9, 80-1, 85, 138
Milner, Bishop John 142
Milner, Sir William 69
Moorman, Bishop John 89, 90, 100
Moverley, Bishop Gerald 111-12
Murphy, Mgr John 112

Newman, Cardinal John Henry 32, 55-6, 84-6, 141-2
Newman College, Birmingham 88
Nolan, Mgr Alban 80
Norfolk, Duke of 126, 130
Norfolk, Duchess of 130

O'Brien, Bishop Kevin 111-12
Oxford 10, 15-26, 150

Paris 14-15
Parker, Dr Tom 21
Parkminster, Sussex 73-5
Pass, Canon Hermann Leonard 23-4
St Paul 89, 119, 149
Paul VI, Pope 76, 81, 85, 92, 93, 102, 104, 105, 120
Peck, David 21
Pensabene Family 51
Peru 123-4
St Peter 87, 116, 117, 119
Pius IX, Pope 22, 128
Pius XI, Pope 23, 33, 43, 105, 120
Pius XII, Pope 76, 103, 104, 120, 150
Pollen, Arther 69
de Porres, St Martin 125
Poskitt, Bishop Henry John 113
Postgate, Bl Nicholas 127
Power, John 108

Quinn, Dr Brian *108*

Radziwill, Princess *70-1*
Ramsey, Archbishop Michael *59*
Ratcliff, Rev E.C. *20*
Reade, Fr Vincent *56*
Rendel, H.S. Goodhart *59*
Renshaw, Noel *21*
Riddle, Michael *21*
Roche, Fr Arthur *12, 122*
Rome, *10, 24, 33-4, 41-8, 81-2, 119, 151*
Rotherstein, Sir John *59*
Row, Mgr Frederick *81*
Ryder, Sue *130*

Saddleworth, Yorks *9*
Sadler, Sir Michael *18*
Salford, Cathedral *15*
Sargeant, Miles *19*
de Satge, Canon *117*
Schmidt, Carl Ludwig *23*
Schutt. Dr Cornelius *45-6*
Shepherd, Bishop David *109*
Soderblom, Archbishop *28*
Spencer, Fr Ignatius *130*
Stone, Dr Darwell *16, 19*
Suenens, Cardinal Leon-Joseph *83, 148*
Sumner, Dom Oswald *35*
Swinton, Lancashire *9*

Tempest Family *126*
Temple, George *58, 61*
Thorne, Canon H.W. *13, 14, 15*
Tomlinson, Mgr George Arther *46, 64*
Trinity and All Saints' College, Leeds *133*
Tristram, Fr Henry *56*

Upholland, St Joseph's College *45, 87, 151*
U.S.A. *62*

Valladolid, English College *48*

Vatican Council Second *75-6, 81-93, 99-105, 115, 116, 150*
Vaughan, Cardinal Herbert *65, 67*
Vavasour Family *127*
Venerable English College, Rome *33, 45, 82*
Vonier, Abbot Anscar *25*

Wales, Prince and Princess of *130*
Walker, Charles *113-4*
Wall, Bishop Bernard *82*
Wallis, Nora *36*
Walters, Canon James E *26*
Wattson, Fr Paul *62*
Waugh, Evelyn *50*
Westminster Abbey *38*
Westminster Cathedral *10, 49, 50, 53-4, 57-60, 63-79, 99, 110, 151*
Wheeler, Frederick *9, 13, 27, 35, 37, 44, 53*
Wheeler, Marjorie *9, 13, 26, 35, 41, 44*
Wheeler, Marjorie Elizabeth ('Betty') *9*
White, Derek *21*
Wicklow, Lady Eleanor *19*
Wilkinson, Fr Tony *123*
Winter, Allen *18*
Wiseman, Cardinal Nicholas *120*
Wodehouse, P. G. *54*
Wodehouse, Roger *20*
Woodall, Hugh *21*
Woodcock, Mr *14*
Woodruff, Douglas & Mia *59*
Worlock, Archbishop Derek *63, 107, 109*
Worsley, Lancashire *9, 13, 15*
Wright, Cardinal John J *51*

York, Archbishop of *90*
York Minster *36, 69*
Yorkshire *126-7*

de Zulueta, Fr Alfonso *68*